BANANA

Edible

Series Editor: Andrew F. Smith

EDIBLE is a revolutionary series of books dedicated to food and drink that explores the rich history of cuisine. Each book reveals the global history and culture of one type of food or beverage.

Already published

Banana

A Global History

Lorna Piatti-Farnell

REAKTION BOOKS

Published by Reaktion Books Ltd
Unit 32, Waterside
44–48 Wharf Road
London N1 7UX, UK
www.reaktionbooks.co.uk

First published 2016

Printed and bound in China by 1010 Printing International Ltd

A catalogue record for this book is available from the British Library

ISBN 978 1 78023 571 4

Contents

Introducing the
Banana Family

Ever since its domestication the banana has played an important part in human history. From its place as a staple food to its cultural part as a symbol of exoticism and colonial power, from its presentation and rebranding as a nutritional wonder to its place at the centre of fair trade controversies, the banana has been entangled with the developments of human history for millennia. The banana is more than just food: it is part of human development and communication. Before the importance of the banana in human lives and histories can be assessed, however, it is necessary to take a journey into the part of the narrative that most consumers are likely to ignore. To put it simply, the physical characteristics of the banana itself: where it comes from, how it grows and what industrial processes provide us with the fruit we recognize today – from plant to plate.

The botanical status of the banana technically classifies it as a berry. In 1977 the botanist James P. Smith curiously described the banana fruit as a 'leathery berry'.[1] Bananas belong to the genus *Musa* and are the product of multiple kinds of herbaceous flowering plants, originating from several parts of the world. The term 'musa' categorizes several genera within the Musacae family; this encompasses a large group of herbaceous flowering plants with leaves that display overlapping basal sheaths, giving the impression of being woody plants. Nonetheless, they are technically regarded as herbs. The banana plant has been called a 'tree' probably throughout its history, in songs, books and popular tales alike; this has done nothing but confuse the issue, and maintained the incorrect myth that bananas come from a tree. It would seem that examples like the popular Rodgers and Hammerstein musical *South Pacific* – originally produced in 1949, providing entertainment and a fair amount of catchy tunes – only continued to cloud the truth, evoking an untouched paradisiacal land where there is an abundance of 'bananas you can pick right off a tree'.[2]

The *Musa* genus counts over 70 species and subspecies and includes, among other things, bananas and their cousin the plantain. Both banana and plantain plants grow high and resemble the anatomy of a tropical tree, with big leaf stalks adding to this common misperception. The banana plant is famously perennial. The above-ground parts of the banana plant flow from a herbaceous structure known as a corm. This is a vertical underground plant stem that primarily operates as a storage organ and is employed by the plant to survive any adverse meteorological conditions, such as winter cold or summer drought. Banana plants are generally tall and robust, their leaves forming a pseudostem (or false stem) that resembles the trunk of a tree. Cultivated banana plants reach various dimensions in height, depending not only on the plant variety, but on the conditions under which they are grown. They are known to be usually around 5 m (16 ft) tall with a number of dwarf varieties being around 3 m (10 ft). Giant versions also exist, which can grow to become 7 m (23 ft) in height or more.[3] The leaves of the banana plant are arranged in a spiral around the stem and may grow to be 2.7 m (9 ft) long and over 60 cm

(2 ft) wide. The leaves are quite brittle and easily frazzled by changes in weather conditions, such as high winds. Once torn, the leaves take on the well-known frond look, giving the banana plant its iconic image.[4]

The process by which the banana plant produces its 'fruit' is similar to that of many other berry-producing plants. When the plant is mature, and has reached its maximum height, the corm stops producing new sets of leaves and begins to form flowers instead. The flower spike forms the stem which, in turn, carries the immature inflorescence that will eventually emerge at the top. Each 'pseudostem' will normally produce only one inflorescence. This 'banana heart' will then develop into the banana itself and take the place of the pseudostem, which will eventually be assimilated into the fruit. The banana 'fruit' comes in a variety of sizes, colours and textures; in general terms, however, the banana can be said to be elongated and curved in shape, with soft and sweet flesh that is often yellow in colour. The flesh is covered by a starch-based rind which may be yellow, green or red and even brown when very ripe.

The image of the unblemished yellow banana is almost universal, especially in the Western world, but it depicts only one type of banana. 'Sweet bananas' – or 'dessert bananas', as they are often referred to in North America and Europe – are the most common type of banana consumed in these areas. They have a softer, less starchy flesh and are primarily eaten raw when ripe. They can also be used for the preparation of sweet and baked dishes. Non-sweet bananas, so defined, are usually labelled as 'plantains'. The term 'plantain' can be used in different ways, but usually refers to a type of banana that is particularly starchy even when ripe and is almost exclusively cooked in order to be consumed, even if very ripe plantains can be consumed raw.[5] In addition to having

Banana inflorescence from a plant in Rarotonga, Cook Islands.

an earthier flavour, plantains have a thicker skin and are more difficult to peel. The general term 'banana' refers to the produce that can be eaten both raw and cooked when it reaches its ripe stage.[6] A cultural differentiation usually sees bananas as 'fruit' and plantains as 'vegetables', even though it is clear that both of these categorizations are incorrect. Although bananas and plantains do mature differently and have very different textures, the primary difference between the two, as far as human interaction is concerned, lies in how they are consumed. Genetically the two are definitely part of the same family. Indeed, in regions outside of America and Europe, such as Southeast Asia, no linguistic differentiation appears to be found between 'banana' and 'plantain'; in these areas multiple and wide-reaching varieties of bananas are grown and consumed, so the overly simplistic twofold differentiation between the two 'types' of banana is redundant.

Bananas are generally grown most successfully in a tropical climate. Although the banana plant prefers a 'wet' soil, it can be grown reasonably successfully as long as good drainage systems and appropriate levels of moisture are maintained, so that the soil remains lush enough in order for the plant to thrive. Ideal soils for the growth of the banana plant are usually deep and well drained, with high humus content, which ensures the fertility of the ground.[7] For these reasons, lands of alluvial or volcanic origin are particularly suitable and preferred for the task of growing bananas. Historically, areas in Malaysia, Indonesia and the islands of the South Pacific have proven to be ideal; however, over time the cultivation of bananas has extended to areas throughout the tropics and, on occasion, even in certain localized areas of the subtropics. Bananas grow best between the temperatures of 20°C and 30°C. Temperatures above 38°C are unsuitable as the excessive heat is known to stop the growth process and even cause the leaves to burn. Similarly the banana plant cannot cope with any form of frost. Chilling damage, which can occur if the plant is exposed to a drop in temperature to below 13°C, can cause extreme damage and eventual death.

Banana clusters are comprised of tiers known as hands and each tier can carry up to twenty fruits. A single banana cluster is known as a bunch and counts several tiers hanging together. Individual banana fruits – the banana itself – are known as fingers, developing on the anatomical metaphor of the hanging cluster. The clusters hang from the top of the plant and often reach the bottom of the shrub area. The anatomy of a banana fruit is rather straightforward, with a protective outer layer – the skin or peel – and numerous strings running down the interior fruit lengthwise. These strings are known as phloem bundles, an unattractive name that curiously recalls the unpleasant feeling that some experience when encountering a string. The inner part of the banana is rich and is said to be composed of 75 per cent water and only 25 per cent solid matter.[8]

The genus *Musa* was formally described for the first time, at least as concerns Western history, by the German-born botanist Georg Eberhard Rumphius in his *Herbarium amboinense* (or *Het Amboinsche Kruidboek*), a catalogue of plants published posthumously in 1741. Rumphius provided ample illustrations and descriptions that were later used by several eminent botanists. At this time the banana was known only by its pseudoscientific, and not appropriately taxonomized, name of *Musa cliffortiana*. The material provided by Rumphius contributed greatly to widely acknowledged works of botanical taxonomy, such as those by Linnaeus. Indeed, it was through Linnaeus' work that the genus *Musa* was formally established. In the first edition of his *Species plantarum*, published in 1753, Linnaeus acknowledged only one type of banana, calling it *Musa paradisiaca* and referring to what is known today as the plantain.[9] At this stage, Linnaeus' categorization of the plant was very simple: he offered a basic description, reporting that this particular cultivar bore long and slender fruits that retained their high starch values, even when cooked. It was not until the publication of his later work *Systema naturae* in 1759 that Linnaeus provided a more elaborate taxonomization of the banana. Even in this later version of his botanical nomenclature, however, he catalogued only two types of banana: *Musa sapientum* for 'dessert bananas' and *Musa paradisiaca* for plantains.[10] It is now acknowledged that these two 'species' are in fact nothing but hybrids, the result of mixtures between *Musa acuminate* and *Musa balbisiana*. The hybridization of banana has been such an important part of the historical development of the fruit we know today that it has often been difficult over time to tell the numerous hybrid types apart.

In spite of its general imprecision, Linnaeus' botanical categorization of the banana remained in wide use for almost two centuries. Careful and meticulous taxonomization of the various banana subgroups did not occur until the 1940s, when researchers such as the English botanist Ernest Entwistle Cheesman cleared up the genetic confusion and gave the banana the scientific attention it deserved. What Linnaeus referred to as *Musa sapientum* is now recognized as closest to the Lantudan cultivar, also known as the 'silk banana'. *Musa paradisiaca* is, on the other hand, most commonly associated with cultivars such as the popular Cavendish (*Musa cavendishii*), named after William Cavendish, the 6th Duke of Devonshire, who gave his patronage to its development in 1834.

Somewhere between myth and scientific fact is the belief that bananas have higher levels of radioactivity compared to other berries and fruits. The idea of a radioactive banana derives from its high potassium content and, in particular, the marginal presence of potassium-40, an isotope with tested radioactivity.[11] Still, even if science confirms the potential radioactive capacities of banana components, no eater should expect visible repercussions from eating the fruit. Dreams of glowing in the dark will sadly not be made true by gorging on mountains of humble bananas.

Banana Varieties

Over 1,000 varieties of bananas exist around the world and they are found in disparate areas of the globe. Not all varieties of bananas are edible, or at least, not all varieties of bananas are commonly produced for consumption. One can still find a large number of wild types of bananas that are inedible, many of which are smaller than a person's little finger and filled with 'tooth-shattering seeds'.[12] Many continue to be cultivated primarily for decorative or ritual use.

Edible, seedless bananas originate mainly from two wild species: *Musa acuminata* and *Musa balbisiana*. Most, if not all, varieties of banana currently grown for consumption can be categorized as hybrids of the two; hybridization, of course, makes for a staggering number of varieties. Most types of edible banana fall within the larger hybrid grouping of *Musa x paradisiaca*, with all its multiple sub-varieties. The differences between varieties are identified not only in relation to physical appearance and conformation, and the obvious culinary uses that come from it, but from their geographical provenance. *Musa balbisiana* is a relatively small group of bananas found

The inside of a wild banana.

The recognizable yellow Cavendish bananas, as sold by the Chiquita company.

primarily in Southeast Asia. The plants of this group of bananas have lush and plump leaves, which are often used in recipes for wrapping and cooking ingredients, especially in Thailand. The subgroups coming under the umbrella of *Musa acuminata* are the greatest in number and represent the majority of the cultivated varieties of banana that are eaten today. These originate primarily from areas of Malaysia, Indonesia, the Philippines, Southern India, East Africa, Thailand, the West Indies, Brazil and Colombia. The list of cultivars within this group is large, with significant levels of genetic diversity.

Musa acuminata favours wet tropical climates, while *Musa balbisiana* is a hardier plant, able to flourish in more adverse weather conditions. Both groups have been subject to human intervention over the centuries, if not millennia. Specimens of the group were introduced in areas where *Musa balbisiana* was known to grow as early as 1000 BC, the mixture of the two resulting in numerous edible and easily transportable banana varieties. Hybridization and the establishment of banana cultivation spread from the Philippines to the Pacific Islands and as far westwards as Africa, reaching the shores of Madagascar via the Indonesian trade around 400 BC.

Yellow bananas, with all their varieties and subspecies, are the most well-known variety of bananas across the globe. Their iconic image and popularity have often caused people to think of this type of banana as the 'real banana'; in truth, the yellow colour does not denote a specific subgroup of bananas, nor even strict botanical differentiation, but is often the result of centuries of engineering and acculturation to make even botanically different and contrasting types of bananas look the same. The commercial reasoning behind this strategy is not difficult to understand.

The variety that most of us in the West are used to eating and therefore commonly recognize as 'the' banana in colour, shape and texture is the Cavendish. This accounts for 47 per cent of the global banana trade, an impressive figure considering the diversity of edible bananas in existence. Cavendish cultivars are distinguished by the height of the plant and features of the fruits, and any slight difference in appearance may be used to quickly categorize an even more specific subgroup. Within the yellow Cavendish subgroup, famous varieties include the Dwarf Cavendish, the Giant Cavendish and the Bluggoe. The Giant Cavendish variety presents a rich and diverse list of cultivars that are actually rather difficult to distinguish, such as the Robusta, the Grande Naine, the Valéry and the *Pisang Masak Hijau*, also known as the Lacatan. The Grande Naine is often credited as being the 'mother' of all contemporary Cavendish varieties, while the Dwarf Cavendish – originating from China – is the most sold variety internationally, since it is hardy and weather resistant.[13]

The Grande Naine has also earned the appellative of 'Chiquita banana', due to its association with the logo and trade of the Chiquita Company. Most varieties of yellow Cavendish bananas are cultivated in Southeast Asia, Central America, the Canary Islands and the West Indies. 'Yellow bananas' are considered ripe when the outer skin reaches the desired yellow colouration, with just a few brown spots.

In spite of its contemporary popularity, the current incarnation of the Cavendish has not always been the favourite. The banana that we love and enjoy today is a relatively recent 'invention' and different even from the variety that our grandparents would have consumed only a few decades ago.[14] The famous banana of the pre-1950s era only marginally resembled our popular Cavendish. This was the *Gros Michel*, literally the 'Big Mike'; it was not only larger, but had a creamier texture and a richer flavour, as well as a visibly thicker skin. For many, this was the 'original' banana, the one that was present on both European and American tables from the late nineteenth century to the few years after the Second World War.[15] It was the *Gros Michel* banana's appearance and distribution, without falling too much into romanticized visions of that era, that came to symbolize the end of the Second World War in many European countries. During this time the banana represented, in a way, a renewed prosperity, its presence confirming the rebirth of commerce and exchange after a time of solemn austerity. Not long after the end of the Second World War, however, the popularity and availability of the *Gros Michel* banana began to diminish. The reason for this was the development of an ailment that affected the banana plants producing this variety; the disease was named after its country of origin and is still known today as the 'Panama disease'.[16] This banana malady is, to be precise, a type of fungus – botanically known as *Fusarium oxysporum* – that is transmitted

Pedro Alexandrino, *Banana and Metal*, c. 1900.

through soil and water and spreads virulently, making the chance of contagion high and the probability of a cure rather low. The Panama disease wiped out most of the banana population grown in Central and South America and Africa, with only a few areas of cultivation surviving in Thailand and Malaysia.

Within the 'green banana' subgroup, one can find primarily the varieties known as 'plantains'. These are large in size, with a distinctive greenish skin. Plantains can actually mature to obtain a yellow colouration, but then are usually considered overripe and of poor quality for cooking due to their mushier texture. In East Africa a popular variety of green banana is the *Musa brieyi*, also known as the East African Highland banana. Uganda is the primary producer of this particular variety, which is, like the majority of banana cultivars, a clone hybrid of *Musa acuminata*, known as the Mutika/Lujugura group.[17] East African Highland bananas – kept rigorously green by

A bunch of green bananas still on the plant, Rarotonga, Cook Islands.

being harvested early – are consumed not only in Uganda but in regions of Tanzania, Rwanda and Burundi. Variations of this type of green plantain are also known to exist in the Caribbean islands.

Within the 'green banana' subgroup, one can also find *Musa basjoo*, commonly referred to as the 'Japanese banana'. Because of its popularity in Japan, this variety of banana was long thought to have originated in the Ryukyu Islands, where the cultivation of *M. basjoo* was first described in local agricultural records.[18] Recent botanical research, however, has identified this type of banana as originating from the Sichuan province in China, where its presence is marked by the growth of both wild specimens and cultivated varieties. It is used predominantly as an ingredient in Chinese medicine. Japanese bananas are not an edible variety; the flesh is sparse and almost completely filled with large black seeds, making their consumption virtually impossible. Instead these bananas are cultivated primarily for ornamental and non-consumptive purposes. As an ornamental plant, *M. basjoo* was developed and grown in Japan in the seventeenth and eighteenth centuries and gained popularity abroad at the end of the nineteenth century, when international trade exchanges between Japan and the West were encouraged and fostered. At this time, the popularity of *M. basjoo* grew in Western Europe, Canada and the United States, where its lush foliage adorned many gardens thanks to its aesthetically pleasing, 'tropical' appeal. In Japan its fibre was also harvested and treated to produce textiles, a practice still in use today. These types of textile are known as *bashōfu*, meaning, literally, 'banana cloth'.[19] The cloth is made by beating, bleaching and drying the whole pseudostem of the banana plant in order to produce a raw material that can be threaded and used to produce items such as tablecloths, kimonos, paper and, most famously, hand-knotted carpets.

Red bananas – also known as Red Dacca bananas in Australia – are a variety of the plant produced in East Africa, South America, the South Pacific and most of Asia. The fruits are small and plump, with the distinctive reddish skin that gives them their name. The flesh of red bananas is cream in colour, with a distinctive pink tinge; the fruits are known to be soft and sweet, almost recalling the taste of raspberries. Technically speaking, red bananas are a subgroup of the Cavendish banana, even though Cavendish bananas are mistakenly thought only to be yellow. Red bananas are also known as claret bananas or Cuban red bananas, the alternative names continuing to pay further homage to the variety's unmistakable red skin.

In the islands of the South Pacific, Fe'i bananas (*Musa troglodytarum*) are a common and preferred variety of the fruit. These have a very distinct appearance from the majority of species of bananas and plantains and have historically derived from a different group of wild species. Fe'i bananas have striking skins, which range from brilliant orange to red in colour, and vivid flesh inside, extending in shade from yellow to orange, often most closely recalling the inside appearance of a mango. Fe'i bananas are known to be rich in beta-carotene, which bestows upon the fruit their vibrant orange colouration; for this reason, this variety of banana is often referred to as a caroteneid banana.[20] They are known to grow upwards inside the pseudostem and are particularly popular in areas such as French Polynesia, the Solomon Islands and Samoa. One of the earliest accounts of Fe'i bananas, at least in Western history, is to be found in the analysis of the genus *Musa* in Rumphius' *Herbarium amboinense* of 1741. In this work the botanist provides a sketch and describes a species of the plant – which he labels *Musa uranoscopos*, or 'heaven-looking banana' – with an upright flowering spike, later producing a fruit with brightly coloured

Red bananas for sale at a tianguis market in Metepec, Mexico State.

flesh. Rumphius also detailed the effects of consuming this fruit on urine, turning it bright yellow, which is consistent with the effects of consuming Fe'i bananas as recorded today. In spite of Rumphius's early effort, an official botanical categorization for Fe'i bananas was not achieved until 1917, when E. D. Merrill proposed a designation for what had been unofficially known by the name *Musa uranoscopos* as the hybrid cultivar of *Musa troglodytarum*. This name, however, was not commonly accepted as an appellative for multiple cultivars of Fe'i bananas until 2004, a very late scientific development as far as botanical categorization goes. It is commonly acknowledged that Fe'i bananas, with their particular red-orange colouration, are the type of fruit portrayed by the artist Paul Gauguin, featured in several of his paintings depicting images of the South Pacific, such as *The Meal*.

A note of caution, of course, is needed in stressing that while colours may vary, this does not necessarily mean either that the bananas themselves are 'different' or that they have very little in common. All varieties of bananas are genetically closely related, their scientific differences being sometimes accredited to very small chromosomic disparities. Taste and texture, however, are a different story, and what are known as close 'banana sisters' may in fact present the potential consumer with a very different experience. In spite of these three colour varieties being the most widely known, it is important

Paul Gauguin, *The Meal*, also known as *The Bananas*, 1891.

to mention that many other differently coloured types of bananas exist, especially outside of the bounds of European and American consumption. The snow banana – also known as *Musa nepalensis* or *Ensete glaucum* – is a larger version of the common Abyssinian banana; commonly grown in areas of Africa, the consumption of this banana variety is peculiar in that it is often grown primarily as a root crop, with the 'fruits' being seen as secondary produce. Pink bananas (*Musa velutina*) are a species of seeded banana grown in multiple tropical areas primarily for their ornamental value, but the sweet flesh can potentially be eaten, if one is brave enough to tackle the hard seeds that are scattered throughout the fruit. Similarly the scarlet banana (*Musa coccinea*) is a variety of banana originating in China and now primarily cultivated in Hawaii, not for eating but purely for its ornamental value.

Cloning and Disease

It would not take long for any potential eater to notice something odd about the inside of the banana fruit: there is a conspicuous lack of seeds. Or, to be precise, the seeds are technically there, but they have been reduced, via centuries of human engineering, to nothing more than tiny black spots. This process has made the banana easy to eat, but has rendered its reproductive functions completely useless. All cultivated bananas are parthenocarpic – sterile fruit incapable of reproducing. One cannot plant a cultivated banana and expect a new plant to grow from it.

The question of how it is possible for banana plants to multiply is answered very simply: by cloning. Bananas reproduce in the same way that works for many other plants (like roses): through a grafting system where parts of the banana plant are replanted to grow thousands of new ones. In this way bananas multiply by the millions, but no real reproduction takes place. Every banana is exactly the same as the next, with the same taste, the same texture, the same colour and virtually the same size. Every banana is a clone of itself. Every banana, as Dan Koeppel suggests, 'is a genetic twin of every other, whether that banana is grown in Ecuador . . . in the Canary Islands . . . or in Australia, Taiwan, and Malaysia'.[21] Bananas are the same everywhere.

It almost goes without saying that just as the cloning process grants the banana the ability to please the consumer with the same experience every time, it also makes every banana equally vulnerable to the potential diseases of its identical siblings. Those diseases cannot be 'cured'. Every plant that is replanted and 'cloned' will carry exactly the same susceptibility to disease as the one it came from; even worse, if the original plant is already infected, the new plants will also be infected and will therefore be doomed to die, as their chances of survival are the same as the original plant: often close to zero.

This is why, when banana species become affected by a destructive disease, entire plantations are destroyed and the species itself can potentially be annihilated and wiped from the pages of agricultural history. This is precisely what happened with the Panama disease that affected the much beloved *Gros Michel* variety. Because of the cloned nature of all banana plants, the disease spread quickly not only in its original location in Panama, but in neighbouring countries such as Guatemala and Costa Rica to the north, even reaching as far as Ecuador and Colombia to the south. And while the process of destruction did not happen overnight, the result was still devastating: within a few decades all plantations were destroyed and by 1960 the *Gros Michel* variety of banana was officially extinct.[22] This was a dark period in the history of the banana trade. Panic spread and it was rumoured that the popularity of the banana had reached its final days, for it is difficult to consume and appreciate a fruit that cannot be found anywhere.

In spite of the gloomy predictions of agricultural experts and the sensationalist headlines to be found in newspapers and on television, the banana did not disappear from supermarket shelves for long. Hope was restored in the form of another banana variety that closely resembled the beloved *Gros Michel*: it was the Cavendish, our contemporary favourite. This variety was seemingly resistant to Panama disease and provided a new alternative to both industry and consumers. Plantations pursued the growth of Cavendish plants instead and this move proved highly successful; in a few years plantations were once again in business and producing even greater crops. The banana industry had been, at least on the surface, saved. The Cavendish banana was hailed as a much stronger variety than its predecessor and consumers were assured that a banana shortage was unlikely to happen again.

In truth, the success of the Cavendish was not attributable to its healthy and strong constitution. Both the Cavendish and the *Gros Michel* are susceptible to Panama disease. The ability of the Cavendish to 'resist' the disease is to be found in the human strategies that were developed around it. In the days of the *Gros Michel*, bananas were only grown in concentrated areas. Even though smaller banana plantations could be found in other areas, most came from Central America. The intermingling of crops was unavoidable. By the time the Cavendish was hailed as the 'new' banana, trade and agricultural systems had changed. Areas of growth were spread to different regions in the world; this was intended not only to avoid the mixing of crops and 'immunize' against disease, but to answer the requirements of a growing global population

Pierre-Auguste Renoir, *The Banana Plantation*, 1881.

who demanded bananas quickly and needed to import them from closer areas. So other geographical zones became a hub for banana plantations, with countries such as Malaysia being apt examples. Less intermingling meant less opportunity for the disease to spread and more of a chance to keep it under control.

And yet, for all the human precautions at work, new incarnations of the Panama disease continue to affect banana plantations around the world. Koeppel estimates that new forms of what is known as 'banana cancer' have the potential to destroy the Cavendish banana population in prolific areas of production, such as Malaysia.[23] This is worrying news not only for the banana industry, but the future of the fruit as we know it. In spite of the devastating nature of Panama disease, it is also important to remember that this is not the only threat posed to banana plants. Innumerable parasites and other botanical maladies are known to attack banana plantations around the world on a regular basis. Cultivated bananas lead a perilous existence, always on the verge of being wiped out. It seems that no matter how hard growers and scientists try, bananas continue to fall sick with numerous maladies and diseases. This is a sad consequence of the results of human engineering on the natural world, where the commercial and cultural success of a product, as far as consumption is concerned, will eventually cause its extinction.

A Note on Etymology

There is a certain lack of clarity on where the term 'banana' actually originated from and much debate on its etymological roots. A commonly accepted explanation, even if the sources are not completely reliable, is that the word 'banana' is thought to be of West African origin, possibly coming from the Wolof term *banaana*. Wolof is a language spoken in Senegal, Mauritania and The Gambia and is the native tongue of the Wolof, a Sub-Saharan ethnic group. It is claimed that the Wolof term was appropriated by Spanish and Portuguese sailors in the sixteenth century and then assimilated into English through the obvious venues for cultural and linguistic exchange that emerge from commercial enterprises and trade. Another etymological explanation claims that the word banana comes from the Arabic *banaana*, meaning fingers, or even *banaan*, meaning fingertips; this explanation may derive from the fact that a bunch of bananas is also known as a hand and that, therefore, calling its fruits fingers would make perfect sense.[24] In truth, there is even less evidence to substantiate this second explanation and the origin of the term 'banana' remains shrouded in mystery. The origin of the English word 'plantain', on the other hand, is firmly rooted in the term *plantano*, the Spanish word for this 'vegetable'.

I

Growing Bananas: Histories, Legends and Myths

In today's global economy, bananas and plantains represent the largest food crop; both their production and their trade exceed that of any other fruit or vegetable on an international scale.[1] In 2006 it was estimated that the total world production of bananas reached 113 million metric tonnes, a huge amount even for a fruit consumed by a high percentage of the global human population. In the islands of Melanesia and Polynesia, as well as in Hawaii, a large proportion of the bananas produced locally are not exported but consumed domestically. Yet areas such as these still managed to produce 17 million metric tonnes destined for the export market and sold internationally. The biggest world producer of bananas is India, with 24 million metric tonnes produced a year, as estimated in 2012.[2] Indian production of bananas, however, is mainly aimed at the domestic market, where the majority of the produce is consumed. Closely following India, the biggest banana producers are China and the Philippines, with Ecuador and Brazil close behind. Other big banana producers, in both the domestic and the export markets, include Guatemala, Uganda, Indonesia and Belize. Recently Australia has been working hard to establish itself as a banana grower;

Bananas for sale at a market in Trivandrum (Thiruvananthapuram), Kerala, India.

banana plantations can be found in the northern tropical regions of the country, just above the state of Queensland.[3] Australian bananas, often of the Cavendish subfamily, are grown in great numbers, but they are primarily consumed domestically in Australia rather than being exported for the international market.

The Banana's Agricultural Beginnings

In his study of the development of the banana trade, Daniel Koeppel contends some of the most successful human efforts in the cultivation of the banana were to be found in the ploughed terraces and gardens of Southeast Asia in 5,000 BC.[4] Ancient historical records show that significant work was put into developing hybridized varieties of the banana plant that would make its fruit fully fit for human consumption. The organized growth of banana crops spread quickly into what is now India, Taiwan and Southern China, Sri Lanka and the Malay Peninsula.

To actually find evidence of the existence of the first banana farms, however, it is necessary to travel to an impenetrable and long-forgotten spot of land that is known as the Kuk Swamp, in the middle of the Wahgi Valley in New Guinea. The area has a small perimeter, but with plentiful grasslands and high humidity levels it is ideal for growing bananas.[5] Archaeological evidence found on the site confirms that 6,900 years ago the area was adapted to the cultivation of bananas. Bacterial research on the ancient soil has revealed that several subfamilies grew in the arable areas of the swamp; the hybridized nature of the fossilized findings suggests deliberate planting and confirms the domestication of the banana plant as an actual crop. This makes the ancient Kuk Swamp not only one of the earliest agricultural sites in the world, but, more specifically, the birthplace of the edible banana as we know it today and the source of its trade and transportation across the globe.[6]

From the Kuk Swamp early examples of domesticated bananas are said to have spread and reached the shores of the Philippines, as the result of early Southeast Asian exploration and commerce. Since its arrival in the Philippines the journey of the banana into other parts of Asia becomes difficult to trace. Researchers of both botany and cultural history have speculated that bananas were taken to several parts of Asia on different voyages, but their popularity as a cultivated fruit did not develop equally in these regions. Therefore, while evidence of bananas being consumed can be found in several parts of Asia, actual plantations took longer periods of time – even centuries – to be established.[7] As a result, the actual geographical development of the banana varieties that we recognize today is difficult to determine. In general terms, it is, however, possible to assert that edible and, later, seedless bananas originated in Southeast Asia and the South Pacific between 8000 and 5000 BC.[8]

Having flourished in the South Pacific and the Philippines, there is abundant evidence that bananas quickly spread and dispersed across all directions in tropical areas. Historical records point us towards the probability that bananas began to be grown in India, Malaysia, Indonesia and even the northern parts of Australia within the first two millennia of being domesticated and grown in the Kuk Swamp. It is clear that with the passing of time the banana plant was domesticated and purposely grown in many parts of the world. Via trade and exchange, bananas settled in Africa – especially in Madagascar – between 3000 BC and AD 100, where agricultural experimentation resulted in other numerous hybrid cultivars that are still currently consumed by African populations.[9] By the third century AD banana plantations were widespread and common in areas of Africa, Asia and the South Pacific. The food historian Alan Davidson claims that bananas reached China in AD 200, where they were mentioned in the writings of Yang Fu; the plants, however, were only grown in the southern regions, where temperatures were warmer.[10]

The shift from the inedible banana to its edible counterpart is indeed a historical marvel, as well as a botanical one. The banana we know today is the result of centuries, if not millennia, of careful mutation, where the varieties with the least seeds were quickly selected, developed and allowed to flourish. The development of the banana as a food for human consumption has therefore been anything but natural: human intervention has made it the fruit it is today. The only thing that has come naturally to the banana as we know it is its ability to find favour among human populations, the same populations that adapted it to their uses and even genetically re-engineered it to have the iconic arc shape that makes it so easy to hold and consume. Bananas were made to be sweeter, their flesh to be softer and easy to chew. Variations were carefully fostered and matured in order to find the ideal incarnation that would suit all members of the population and which could be used, in one way or another, in a variety of dishes, both savoury and sweet. It was the effort of skilful agricultural masters that, over time, transformed a wild and often inaccessible foodstuff into a staple food of the human diet in different parts of the world, an amazing accomplishment that has very little to do with the divine, but speaks instead of hard work and commitment.

Bananas in the Ancient World

The appearance of the banana as both a food and a crop is only scantily documented in the ancient world. Ancient Egyptian hieroglyphics and carved drawings dating from 1000 BC show evidence of the banana being consumed; records also show that the ancient Egyptians used banana leaves, fruit and the flowering sheaths as wound dressings, often mashing the fruit and applying it to grazes and rashes in the form of a poultice.[11] The presence of bananas in ancient Egypt, however, has never been fully investigated; the only certainty seems to be that the bananas consumed in ancient Egypt were Abyssinian in origin. The botanical historian Khair Al-Busaidi also reports that the Assyrian civilization, which extended its dominion into the regions of the Nile, may have consumed bananas and introduced them to regions of the Middle East as early as the eleventh century BC.[12] These reports, however, are not fully documented and often rely on sources that only possibly refer to the banana and its consumption.

To find a historically accurate description of bananas, one must wait until the fourth century BC. It is rumoured that, during their campaign in India, the soldiers of Alexander the Great spotted banana trees growing. It was during this time that the first mentions of the banana began to appear in the writings of the learned men who travelled with the emperor's expedition into the East. The Greek philosopher and historian Theophrastus, who travelled to the Far East with Alexander's armies, gave a detailed description of the banana in his analysis of botanical specimens, *Historia plantarum* (An Enquiry into Plants).[13] Mention of the banana appears in Theophrastus' work in relation to his brief discussion of Indian plants, set primarily against Greek and Egyptian plants of the time. In his botanical treaty he does not specifically name the plant or its fruit and only incorporates it into a list of 'other fruits' that in his opinion resembled – to some extent or another – plants already known in ancient Greece, such as the banyan. Theophrastus refers to the plant as having 'leaves that resemble in shape the wing of a bird, being three cubits in length, and two in breadth'.[14] The plant, Theophrastus goes on to say, 'puts forth its fruit from the bark, a fruit remarkable for the sweetness of its juice, a single one containing sufficient to satisfy four persons'.[15] Even though Theophrastus clearly applied some poetic licence in describing this particular plant, undoubtedly designed to entice the curiosity and fascination of his readers at home, later references to the fruit's green and yellow skin and its pulpous flesh leave no doubt in connecting this mysterious text to the banana. In spite of the clear interest in the exotic Indian plant, however, the Greeks failed to transport the fruit back to their homeland and the banana – at least for a while – remained in the margins of Greek travel lore.

Centuries later, in the Roman world, the natural philosopher Pliny the Elder also recognized the importance of the banana in his famed *Natural History*, an encyclopaedic collection written in AD 77 in which he discusses most of the knowledge of the time in the fields of botany, zoology, mineralogy, astrology and geology. The connection between bananas and India is again picked up by Pliny: he describes the fruit as being one the favourite foods of cultured men, going so far as to claim that only 'the sages dine on it'. In the eighteenth century, when Linnaeus, 'the Father of Taxonomy', catalogued bananas in his detailed categorization of plants, he gave them a scientific name that was clearly a homage to the fruit's naturalist and cultural legacy as the food of sages: he named it *Musa sapientum*, the 'fruit of wise men'. Like the ancient Greeks, the Romans did not show particular interest in introducing the banana into their daily diet and failed to pick up on its nutritious potential and its widely accessible nature.

In his *Origin of Cultivated Plants*, published in 1886, the French botanist Alphonse De Candolle firmly maintained that it was highly improbable, virtually impossible, for the same genus of banana cultivars to have been developed in two widely separated parts of the world. This is owing to the fact that edible bananas can only reproduce in a vegetative manner and not by the planting of seeds. De Candolle's statement still rings true today; therefore, in order to attempt a geographical tracking of the banana from Asia to the Middle East and then Europe, one needs to focus attention not on the plants' 'natural' spreading, but on distinctly human means such as commerce. Indeed, the Arab/Swahili and Malay trade played a vital role in the early dispersal of the banana across regions of the Indian Ocean and into the Arab world. Historical records indicate that the introduction of banana crops into the Arabian Peninsula at this stage was intensive. In the first millennium BC similarities could be found between the bananas consumed in the Persian Gulf and those found in Southeast Asia, especially in the Indus regions.[16] Archaeological evidence of the spread of the banana at this time is still limited and the exact route of the banana into the Middle Eastern region is difficult to track and still open to speculation. To find actual recorded evidence of cultivation in the Arabian Peninsula, one must wait until the early medieval period.[17] The inconsistencies between records in ancient agricultural practices – some claiming that the banana was widespread in the Arabian Peninsula in the BC centuries and others maintaining that it was not cultivated until the early centuries AD – make a definitive answer on the journey of the banana into the Middle East difficult to obtain.

Nevertheless, there is reason to believe that bananas were consumed in what is recognized today as the Yemen region as early as the ninth century BC, a result of the Arabic forays into Asia. In spite of its popularity in the Arabian Peninsula, as well as regions of Africa, the introduction of bananas into the West would have to wait until after AD 600, when the spread of Arab commerce during the Islamic expansion made the fruit a staple of the everyday food regimen, for those who could afford it.[18] By the beginning of the thirteenth century bananas were known to have spread to multiple areas of North Africa, reaching as far as Moorish-ruled southern Spain.[19]

Into the West

In the fifteenth century Portuguese sailors, and later traders, transported the first bananas from West Africa to the Canary Islands, where the first plantations of European roots were known to have originated. Banana plantations can still be found on the Canary Islands today, producing large quantities of the bananas consumed in Europe. The Portuguese also established numerous crops of bananas in Brazil, and it is believed that it was from here that the banana spread into the Caribbean, where it became part of local commercial exchanges, as well as the cultural fabric of the everyday. By the sixteenth century banana production in the Caribbean had become connected to the economy of colonial plantations. In 1516, when the Catholic missionary Friar Tomás de Berlanga reached the island of Hispaniola – today Haiti and the Dominican Republic – he was said to have planted banana plants in an effort to provide a cheap source of food for the growing local African slave population.[20] Bananas proved to be a highly effective source of nourishment for the slaves, which, much to the masters' delight, also came with inexpensive maintenance and production costs. In the inner cosmos of the Caribbean plantations many uses were found for the banana plants and, consequently, their fruits.

At this time the banana was not the centre of any commercial activities, or, at least, not as a direct commodity. The value of the fruit as an international commodity had not yet been capitalized upon. The most common use for the banana plant was as an intercropping device. The popular crops of cacao, coffee and peppermint in the colonial islands relied upon indirect sunlight in order to flourish, and unfortunately the Caribbean sun continuously provided direct sunlight that was often detrimental to their growth. Banana plants, on the other hand, with their wide and towering leaves, would offer the perfect amount of shade and protection to the crops that were actually being sold.[21] The use of the fruit as food for the slaves in the plantation was only secondary to the plant's primary role in aiding the growth of other precious crops. Still, the importance of the banana as an inexpensive and easy-to-grow source of nourishment continued to be acknowledged and exploited for decades, if not centuries. The variety of bananas grown during this time would have actually been what is recognized today as the plantain, which offered a much starchier source of nourishment for the slaves. Plantains were highly digestible and provided a copious amount of calories, necessary for carrying out tasks that required high-intensity manual labour. The banana plant was therefore a valuable part of the colonial plantation economy, not as a sellable product, but as an integral part of the growing infrastructure.

As well as introducing the cultivation of banana plants to the Caribbean islands, Friar Tomás is also credited with being the first person to take bananas to the American continent in the sixteenth century. When he moved to Panama and was appointed bishop, Friar Tomás took samples of banana plants with him, allowing them to spread across the mainland. It was not long before bananas became a favourite, and reasonably cheap, source of food for the local population; the plants grew quickly and produced abundant quantities of nutritious fruit. Banana plantations, as a result, appeared and flourished across the greater parts of Central America and Mexico, and the popularity of the fruit spread even more widely – so much so that, as the food historian Victoria Scott Jenkins claims, 'later observers believed the banana to be native to the New World.'[22]

The first English colonists arriving in the North American continent and landing in Roanoke Island, just off the coast of what is now North Carolina, are said to have brought bananas with them that they had collected on their journey through the Caribbean. The initial intention of the colonists is said to have been to set up plantations of the fruit and turn the endeavour into a profitable business venture. The banana plants, however, struggled with the local weather, as bananas are not able to thrive outside of tropical climates. Other early

William Berryman, 'Plantain Walk', early landscape of Jamaica, 1808–16, watercolour, pencil and black ink.

nineteenth-century attempts to grow bananas on the North American mainland, known to be localized in the warmer areas of modern-day California and Florida, were also recorded to be unsuccessful.[23] On the other hand, bananas were found to be growing in the Hawaiian islands when the famed Captain Cook visited in 1799.

Before the 1800s bananas were rare in the United States, as well as Europe, and virtually no one living in the country had ever eaten, or even seen, a banana.[24] This does not mean, of course, that bananas were not to be found on sale at speciality shops in the United States and Europe; indeed, bananas were available to buy, but remained a clear luxury, reserved for the wealthy of the age. A sudden interest in the banana was sparked when Jules Verne gave a description of it in his popular novel *Around the World in 80 Days*, published in 1873, calling it 'as healthy as bread and as succulent as cream'.[25] Even with this literary reference, however, the popularity of the fruit on a grand scale did not seem to grow. Bananas spoiled fast and the lack of appropriate transportation methods made their sale a difficult endeavour.

Nonetheless, the development of new travel technologies in the late nineteenth century changed the fate of the banana completely, affecting not only its availability but its popularity in the United States as well as Europe. In America the introduction of steamships began a process of food transportation that would soon change the way in which bananas were made accessible to the general public forever. But the real innovation in terms of transport and availability came, unsurprisingly, in the form of the railway. This extremely functional means of travel made transportation easy and quick, so that bananas could be made available in every corner of the United States.[26] The invention of the railway, coupled with faster moving ships and new and improved refrigeration techniques, allowed bananas to transform from an exotic and inaccessible luxury commodity to an everyday staple. As a result, the u.s. is known to have imported over 16 million hands of bananas from Central America and the Caribbean islands over a period of a few years. In 1876 the price of a single banana on the East Coast of the u.s. was estimated to be 10 cents, equivalent to a 1.5 litre bottle of milk. This was quite a revolutionary step for a tropical food that had previously been the domain of the rich. In the late 1880s different varieties of bananas, from yellow to red, were made readily available to consumers in the major city markets of New York, Boston and Philadelphia.[27]

By the turn of the twentieth century bananas had become a common presence in all markets across the country, even if their price varied and often increased the further one travelled towards the West Coast. In 1905 Charles Q. C. Leigh founded the Leigh Banana Case Company, whose great innovation was the patent of a new container for transportation: a wood-veneer slatted crate that was built specifically to fit one bunch of bananas. In spite of their custom-built nature, these

Banana carriers in Cameroon, 1912.

crates took up a lot of space, and as new patents for fruit containers developed in the 1930s sales of the Leigh banana cases started to decline.[28] It probably did not help that the Leigh banana case somewhat resembled a medieval torture device rather than a box for banana cargo. On the other side of the Atlantic a similar situation manifested: refrigerated transportation by means of railway and steamships made bananas a common fruit in European markets, with England and Germany leading the way as the principal banana consumers. It is estimated that by the late 1900s over two million hands of bananas had been imported into Germany. Later, refrigeration trucks were introduced into the food transport industry in the late 1940s, and increased the sales of bananas to those of the 'common fruit' we recognize today.[29]

In the 1920s, at a time when the popularity of bananas was increasing in the United States and Europe, heavy propaganda was circulated by fruit companies to convince consumers that eating the fruit was necessary for maintaining a healthy lifestyle. Children, as well as athletes, were particularly targeted as being in need of the essential sugars and vitamins provided by bananas. The message was clear to all: a healthy diet would include a sizeable dose of bananas, with one a day being the recommended dose. The health-conscious members of the middle and upper classes would quickly take to eating bananas regularly and the popularity of the fruit, as well as the profits for the fruit companies, continued to increase. Bananas were advertised as – and commonly considered to be – virtually impervious to most germs and bacteria. Deemed a 'safe food' to consume all year round, the use of bananas was introduced into medical practices and they were sold as a sanitary treatment for a number of maladies. By the 1930s bananas were prescribed by medical practitioners, both in America and in Europe, for the treatment of diarrhoea, colitis, malnutrition and even tuberculosis.[30] In 1931 the American Medical Association went as far as proclaiming the banana an essential part of the public's diet. Very little evidence was given for the banana's effective medical properties; indeed, to think that a banana could actually provide any actual cure, or even relief, for the deadly malady of tuberculosis seems absurd. Still, the fruit's proven high levels of vitamins and other good nutrients, like minerals, was enough to convince the public that bananas were a remedy for illness and an important part of any health regime.

Transport crates for the Leigh Banana Case Company, c. 1910.

A New York street vendor's cart with bananas on sale, 1906

Myths, Legends and Folklore

Throughout history numerous examples of mythology and legend have featured the banana as an element in the ways in which the gods manifest and make their presence known to humans. Bananas are often conspicuously connected to myths of how things on Earth were created and how they have impacted on the human way of life. Stories of this nature can be found copiously scattered throughout the mythological heritage of countries around the world, from areas of Africa to the Middle East and Asia, and often centre on narratives of the paranormal and the divine. In the central regions of Indonesia, for instance, the people of Poso tell the story of 'The Stone and the Banana', of how the Creator commonly sent objects and ideas down to the first people, using a rope that he lowered from his sky home.[31] One day, wanting to offer people a chance to gain immortality, he lowered down a stone. Seeing it as useless, the people foolishly rejected it. Surprised by the refusal, the Creator then lowered a banana instead and people quickly ran to grab it. At this, the Creator scolded the stupidity of the humans, explaining that had they accepted the stone they would have achieved solidity and therefore eternal life, but, having picked the banana instead, they had chosen hard work, hardship and mortality and therefore introduced death into the world.

The similarities between the Indonesian myth of the banana and the stone and the narration of Adam and Eve's fall from grace in the Garden of Eden are undeniable. Both stories point in the direction of people choosing to eat a fruit and thereby denying the authority and gifts of a higher divine power. However, if the similarities seem less obvious because the Judaeo-Christian, and later Islamic, tale of Adam and Eve clearly put an apple at the centre of the deadly choice, it might be compelling and rather surprising to learn that the fruit that Eve picked may actually have been something that closely resembled a banana. According to the myth, God gifted Adam and Eve with a garden full of abundance and gave them free access to everything their eyes beheld. This gift came with only one condition: they could eat anything apart from the fruit that came from 'the tree of knowledge of good and evil', with the warning that eating from it would bring them certain death. It is commonly acknowledged that the fruit in question was an apple, but some contemporary scholars have recently argued that this may in fact be based on a mistranslation of the original text when it was translated into Latin. Many of the ancient biblical texts, written in Hebrew and then Greek, never specifically identified the 'fruit of knowledge' as an apple.[32] Historical records now show that this common conception actually emerged around the year AD 400, when St Jerome created the Vulgate Bible, the first text that made the scripture available to a wider audience. Jerome's Latin Bible was later chosen as the version utilized by Johannes Gutenberg in 1455, when the printing press made the text even more widely available to the faithful. Jerome used Latin as his idiom of choice and, like many other languages, including English, Latin is known to have many words that sound or are even spelled the same but which have completely different meanings. When Jerome was presented with the task of translating the ancient Hebrew word for 'evil' he chose the Latin *malum*, which was intended as meaning something more closely related to the term 'malicious'.[33] *Malum*, however, can also be translated as 'apple', a term derived from the ancient Greek word for the fruit. It is rumoured that when artists in the early Renaissance used the printed Latin Bible as a term of reference for their craft, they did not question the misrepresentation of *malum* as 'apple' and therefore began painting the fruit as the one picked by Eve in the Garden of Eden. The reference to the fruit as an apple has been debated over centuries of scholarship, and many have asserted that the fruit of the tree of knowledge should in fact have been identified as a banana.

Linnaeus is said to have been a firm believer in this different interpretation. Many claim that evidence for this can be found in his designation of the banana into the family he called *Musa*, which derives from the Arabic word *mauz*, meaning banana. This designation is reinforced by the fact that the Koran identifies the banana as belonging to the original Garden of Eden.[34] In this text the forbidden tree is known as *talh*, the ancient Arabic word that is commonly translated as 'tree of paradise' – and, on occasions, even more explicitly as 'banana tree'. The Koran offers a description of the tree of knowledge as having 'fruits piled one above the other, in long extended shade . . . whose season is not limited'. There is certainly no doubt that the description offered in this Islamic text closely resembles that of the physical appearance of the banana plant and its fruit. The connection between Muslim and Judaeo-Christian interpretations of the Garden of Eden and the fruits of the tree of knowledge naturally intersect. And even though their dogmatic interpretations went in separate directions, one must consider the likelihood of the texts

Giorgio de Chirico, *The Uncertainty of the Poet*, 1913.

including examples from the botanical landscape that would have been known to the biblical and Koran writers of the time. The banana would have been a much more likely choice for the depiction of the forbidden fruit, as those living in the Middle East would have been familiar with the fruit and its exotic, 'paradisiac' qualities.[35] This is not to assert, of course, that the fruit described in the myth of the Garden of Eden can undoubtedly be identified as the banana; nonetheless, it is fascinating to consider a different version of the famous story that includes the banana at the centre of the narrative, especially if one considers the persuasive evidence that exists for this idea.

Several other mythological stories, especially those focusing on matters of the supernatural, include the banana prominently, always connected to some form of cautionary tale in relation to spirits, ghosts or gods. In Thailand nature spirits known as the 'lady banana ghosts' reportedly live within small banana trees.[36] The spirits are said to be reluctant to leave their trees without provocation; however, they can become angry if they are forcibly made to leave and will take out their vengeance on the humans who unwittingly cause their displeasure. The spirits will use their magic to frighten the humans and keep them away, but never really cause them harm. They are said to be particularly favourable towards travelling monks, to whom they will present gifts. The lady banana ghosts are believed to be at the peak of their powers when the banana plants are glowing with luscious flowers. The banana here appears to be an allegorical warning against human destruction or disturbance of the natural world, with the banana spirits punishing those who do not respect it. It is not surprising to see the banana picked for such a task, considering its undeniable importance in the culinary and cultural structures in Thailand.

In Hawaii a well-known legend focused on the interactions between humans and gods is that of 'The Strange Banana Skin'. This tale tells the story of Kukali, who lived hundreds of years ago in the days of the Polynesian migration. Kukali was known to have visited many strange islands and to have accomplished many great feats. This glorious and adventurous life was achieved thanks to the power of a banana skin.[37] Kukali's father, who was a priest, was said to have given him a magical banana, and instructed his son to keep the skin after he ate the fruit. Kukali took the banana on his adventures, and every time hunger came and he consumed the fruit, the empty skin would magically fill up with banana flesh again. Kukali was careful not to lose or throw away the banana skin, taking it on his travels to faraway lands, hungry with the desire for discovery. One evening Kukali fell into a deep slumber after his daily meal of banana; while he was asleep, he was flown away by the great god-bird Halulu. The bird intended to devour the young man and for this reason took him to his nest. When Kukali awoke he found himself in the company of other sailors who had been kidnapped and who would soon be turned into Halulu's feast. Kukali, however, used his eternally self-regenerating banana to feed the prisoners and make them strong again. He taught them how to make weapons and how to attack the feathers of the god-bird in order to escape. When Halulu returned to the nest, ready for his feast, Kukali and the other prisoners fought him and broke his wings into many pieces. The story is said to end with Kukali finding extra courage after killing the god-bird and conquering the lands presided over by Halulu's sister goddess Namakaeha and her *kahunas* (priests). All this time, Kukali's strength was renewed by the flesh of the magical banana. After his great battles Kukali is said to have returned home and married the local chieftess, who granted him the power to rule over the lands in

Hawaii. One can see here how the magical properties of the banana are an allegorical representation of its role as a staple in the Hawaiian diet, providing nourishment and supporting the population as it grows and flourishes. The story of Kukali and his enchanted skin uncovers the banana as an important cultural presence in Hawaiian heritage, the reflection of human ingenuity and bravery, and the likely symbolic core of local social, political and economic organization.

Throughout the symbolic narratives of the global imagination there are also several examples in tales of folklore where the banana figures prominently. These tales are often allegorical and fable-like in nature, usually including anthropomorphic characters whose adventures provide an explanation of everyday matters, as opposed to spiritual and divine ones. A well-known example of this is the story of 'The Monkey and the Turtle', originating from the Philippines. In this tale, the monkey and the turtle find a banana plant and divide it equally between themselves. The monkey, thinking itself clever and cunning, chooses the upper end of the plant for itself, claiming all the leaves, while the turtle is left with the roots. The plant is cut in half, and each animal plants its share into the ground. However, when the time to collect the fruits comes, only the turtle's half has given bananas, while the monkey's half has withered and died. As the turtle cannot climb to the top of the plant, it asks the monkey to help to collect the fruit. The monkey agrees, but instead of collecting the fruit as promised, it eats all the ripe bananas, mocking the turtle by throwing only a few green and unripe ones to the ground. Infuriated by being cheated, the turtle places a sharp shard of bamboo under the banana plant and as the monkey climbs down, it impales itself on the bamboo and is killed.[38]

If this initial part of this story seems only relatively gory, the final part makes it positively horrific. After ensuring that his enemy is definitely dead, the turtle chops the monkey's body into small pieces, salts it to perfection and then leaves it in the sun to dry, ready to eat. The turtle then travels to the nearby mountains and sells the delicious meat to the local monkey tribe, who devour it and ask for more. At this, the turtle laughs and mocks the monkeys for eating their own flesh. Multiple endings exist to the story, and all seem to conclude with the turtle, one way or the other, getting the better of the monkeys, who try with multiple stratagems to enact their revenge.[39] Although it might come across as a little gruesome, especially to Western sensibilities, the story of the monkey and the turtle is commonly used in Filipino folklore to explain why monkeys don't eat meat, preferring bananas instead. The banana represents both safety and an important commodity to be cherished and looked after, explaining the common appearance of the banana in various Filipino recipes, for reasons that go beyond simple availability.

In Indonesia many folk tales involve allegorical animals interacting with bananas, as well as other fruits. Famous examples of this are the stories of Kanchil, the much beloved trickster of Indonesian folklore who resembles an animal somewhere between a mouse and a deer. In a story called 'The Sacred Banana Leaf', for instance – one of many adventures in which Kanchil uses bananas for his purposes – the trickster falls into a pit. With only a banana leaf at his disposal, he cunningly invents a prophecy according to which the leaf is actually 'sacred' and will protect him in the inevitable eventuality of the world ending. Kanchil uses the leaf to trick some unsuspecting animals into helping him out and then following his instructions, for fear of dire consequences. The reverence for the banana as a quasi-mystical fruit, mixed with the devotion to its place in Southeast Asian culinary practices, is visible in this story, as is the recognition of the importance

Attributed to Hans Looschen, *Ape with Bananas*, 1923.

the banana plays in local cultural narratives. A recent retelling of the traditional folk story can be found in Nathan Kumar Scott's illustrated version of *The Sacred Banana Leaf* (2008), where the spiritual importance of the banana is Indonesia is clearly recognizable.[40]

The banana also appears in uncountable folk tales on the other side of the globe, where varieties of bananas have also been grown for centuries. In the Caribbean numerous stories of creativity, buoyancy and a fair dose of mischief are centred on dealings with bananas. In the Bahamas, for instance, stories of the beloved character of 'Rabbit' often portray him trying to acquire a 'big bunch ripe banana' for himself. The bananas always come to represent the local spirit of ingenuity.[41] In Jamaica, folklore a popular story is that of 'The Tar Banana tree'. The story tells of a wealthy businessman who owns a banana plantation. Every night, a thief enters the plantation and steals bananas. After the thievery has continued for a long period of time, the angry plantation owner – the 'Boss' in the folktale – decides to entrust to Brer Anancy, one of his faithful workers (often portrayed as a wily spider and a popular folk hero in Jamaica), the task of catching the thief. Unbeknown to the owner, Anancy is actually the banana thief, so the search turns out to be predictably unsuccessful. Disappointed with his worker's failure to carry out the task, the 'Boss' decides to take matters into his own hands and paints all the banana plants with tar, hoping to catch the elusive thief. On that same night, when Anancy tries to steal himself a pretty bunch of bananas, his hands remain stuck on the surface of the plant and prevent him from escaping. Panicked, Anancy calls for the help of 'Brer Nanny Goat', a passing simpleton. However, in the commotion of pulling and pushing, Brer Nanny Goat becomes stuck to the plant, while Anancy is able to pull free. Upon being freed, Anancy ties up Brer Nanny Goat and accuses him of being the banana thief. Upon the arrival of the owner Brer Nanny Goat is questioned on his thievery, but in his panic he fails to accuse Brer Anancy, and only manages to mutter 'Brer-bre-bre . . .' over and over. The story ends with a lesson, claiming that this is the reason why goats and rams are known to only utter 'brer-bre-bre' instead of speaking.[42] This Jamaican tale once again places the banana at the centre of a story explaining an everyday occurrence with a mythologized origin. It is no surprise that the banana should occupy such a central place in folklore stories of the everyday, as the fruit itself has been the centre of both leisure and work life in the Caribbean, as well as other areas, for centuries.

2

How to Eat Bananas

Until the nineteenth century in most of Europe and the United States, bananas were primarily eaten raw as a snack food or served with several types of dessert.[1] This was a method of consumption reserved, of course, for sweet bananas, and is still one of the most common ways to eat this type of fruit to the present day. By 1900, however, bananas were being used in experimental dishes that required different levels and types of preparation. Variations on cooked and processed bananas of the time included fried banana fritters, banana ice cream and even bananas served with meat; this latter 'experiment' was only new to Western plates, as bananas had been commonly used in savoury dishes in Asia for centuries.

Today banana creams, custards, ice creams and puddings – and even simply cooked banana 'chips' – are common and favoured dishes in the United States as well as other parts of the world. *Larousse gastronomique* claims that 'cooking bananas brings out their full flavour', especially when combined with 'sugar, butter or alcohol'.[2] Banana puddings are particularly favoured in the southern United States, where they overtook English trifle in popularity at the end of the nineteenth century and became a popular addition to local cookbooks. *Mrs Rorer's New Cook Book*, published by Sarah Tyson Rorer in

1902, contained a recipe for banana pudding, together with other banana recipes such as baked bananas and banana cake. Mrs Rorer conspicuously classified banana pudding as a 'Hawaiian recipe'. In 1903, however, when Mary Harris Frazer published her own recipe for banana pudding in *The Kentucky Receipt Book*, the dish was openly acknowledged as an 'American' dessert.

During the same period a penchant was also discovered in the United States and Britain, as well as South Africa, for eating bananas for breakfast; at this time well-known cereal companies began to advertise the consumption of the fruit as

Banana guard, a gadget for transporting and protecting bananas, introduced in the 20th century.

a suitable accompaniment to the cereal. The marriage between banana and breakfast cereal was joyous and profitable, experiencing a resurgence in the advertising campaigns of the 1950s and '60s. This preference remains alive today, and bananas are often presented as an ideal topping for breakfast cereals, with brands such as Kellogg's continuing to emphasize the advantages of the combination. Banana beverages also began to be advertised and proliferated, especially those that were hot alternatives to coffee-based drinks. Examples like Banan-Nutro, which experienced huge popularity at the beginning of the twentieth century, are testament to the ways in which bananas quickly colonized the eating habits and preferences of the Western world.

In the majority of countries and cuisines in the West, cooked bananas are served predominantly in desserts and sweet dishes. In countries such as the United States and the United Kingdom, bananas are primarily used in recipes for breads, cakes and muffins. Bananas can even be wrapped foil and roasted on the barbecue as a sweet treat, a method of preparation known as 'banana boats'. Well-known banana dishes see the fruit served flambé, au gratin, in soufflés and even with bacon for breakfast.[3] In the late 1970s the A. J. Canfield Company of Chicago produced the Anna Banana Soda, a carbonated drink with a strangely manufactured banana flavour. It was not a hit with consumers; the taste was just too odd and unpleasant, and what might have worked for custards and puddings definitely did not work for a carbonated drink. Canfield were forced to retire the product early, with multiple crates of unopened sodas cluttering their warehouses. Bananas also often see their shape replicated in sweets and

Cover of a Fyffes Bananas Cookbook from the UK, c. 1900.

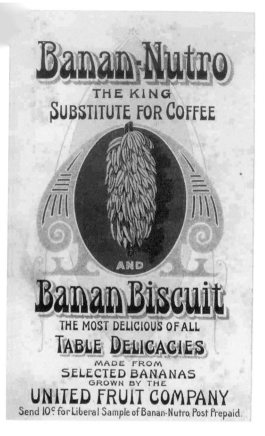

candy; the commonly known 'foam bananas' have been a favourite with children and adults alike for decades. These banana sweets, however, seem to have a rather artificial banana flavour, resembling more closely a chemical and lab-designed taste and smell of bananas, rather than the natural taste and smell of the fruit. The high sugar – together with the obvious fact that bananas are not an ingredient in the recipe – is most likely the culprit in this taste crime. The same can be said for the popular 'banana' ice-lollies.

Nutri-Banane tin, early 20th century.

Védrenne sirop, as sold in France, in both green and yellow banana flavours.

Many culinary uses for the banana – often in its incarnation as the plantain – can be found around the world. In Southern India and areas of Southeast Asia, including Malaysia and Indonesia, as well as most parts of the Caribbean, the starchier plantains are used as a cooking ingredient in a number of savoury dishes.[4] In other areas, such as Thailand, banana plant leaves are used as a casing for other foods such as rice and fish, and commonly employed as a steaming receptacle. In tropical regions bananas are consumed as the staple starch and are therefore used as a primary ingredient in a variety of everyday dishes, from breakfast to dinner. In Uganda and Tanzania, the East Highland version of the plantain is commonly mashed or pounded into meal, which is cooked in a variety of dishes.[5] The most common of these is *matoke* – also known as *matooke*, or *ebitookye* in southern Uganda – a traditional dish made out of the steam-cooked and mashed

Foam banana sweets.

Matoke served with chicken.

meal of the green plantain. *Matoke* is a staple dish of the Ugandan diet, and is often eaten with meat or smoked fish, served in green banana leaves, which also act as the bowl.

Throughout India bananas are used in a variety of both savoury and sweet dishes. Curries in particular often use bananas in a savoury combination. Many of these specialities actually call for what is known as 'raw banana'; if this wording may seem strange to untrained cooks, it will be a relief to learn that this is just another name for plantain. *Vazhakkai* curry, for instance, is a South Indian speciality in which raw bananas are mixed with coconut oil, curry leaves and other dry ingredients, such as turmeric, coriander seeds and *urad dal*, to create a spicy vegetarian dish. Another well-known raw banana dish originating from South India – the Andhra region in particular, where Telugu cuisine is predominant – is *arartikaya podi koora*, a roasted raw banana curry made with the additional flavours of ginger and cumin seeds. In the northern regions of the country, raw banana-based dishes have a distinctly sweeter flavour; examples from local curry recipes such as raw banana *kofta* show a clear prevalence for adding ingredients such as cinnamon, paneer and cashews, adding to the creamy textures and flavours for which North Indian curries are famous. The list of raw banana curries in India is long and varied. In spite of the differences, however, all these dishes pay testament to the important part that the banana – or the plantain – has played in the cultural history of the country, placing itself at the core of its culinary heritage. The importance of the banana in Indian cuisine can be also

Banana *halwa* in South India.

seen in its prevalence in accompaniments and sweet dishes. An example of this is *tarela kera*, hard 'chips' made from yellow bananas – not plantains – that are cut into thin slices, shallow fried in ghee and served either as an accompaniment to curry dishes or on their own as a snack. On the sweet front, the list of banana-based recipes is rich; a notable example is *halwa*, a delicacy from Mangalore, made with ripe yellow bananas, with the addition of sugar and lemon juice, and commonly served during celebrations such as weddings.

India, however, is not the only country to have capitalized on the versatility of both sweet bananas and plantains in its local cuisine. Countries such as Thailand, Indonesia and Malaysia count almost innumerable examples of banana dishes in their culinary repertoires, marking the legacy of Southeast Asia as one of the banana's places of origin. In Indonesia, for instance, one can consume the popular *jumput jumput*, a type of banana fritter, or *pisang bakar saus kinca*, a recipe of green plantain in plum sugar sauce. In Malaysia one can find *goreng pisang* (curiously known as *pisang goreng*

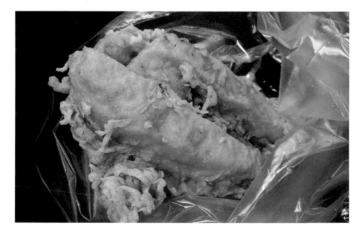

Fried banana fritters, also known as *goreng pisang* in the Malay language.

Ghanaian-style fried plantains.

in Indonesia), fried bananas that are usually sold by street vendors as a form of fast food. This type of fried banana is usually coated in rice flour and coconut and then fried just enough to become crispy on the outside. A similar dish is also served in Thailand, under the name *kluay tod*. Thailand is another country that has made a virtue of the banana as an ingredient in its dishes, in particular utilizing the leaves of the banana plant to wrap up fish and other ingredients before cooking. The banana leaves impart a subtle and delicate flavour to their filling while also protecting it from being burned. A popular dish of this kind, also known in regions of Laos and China, is *khao dome*, coconut sticky rice wrapped in banana leaf. Thai cuisine also includes several sweet recipes that include the banana as a prominent ingredient, such as *khao tom madt*, sweet bananas in sticky rice.

In a completely different geographical region, that of Central and South America and the Caribbean, bananas and plantains are also an important part of the local cuisines. This recurrent presence should not come as a surprise, considering that all these areas have both a historical and ongoing relationship with growing, selling and consuming varieties of the fruit. In Puerto Rico one can taste *viandas con bacalao*, salted cod cooked with tropical root vegetables, including plantain. In Ecuador a popular dish is *maduros asados*, a dish of matured plantains, which can be prepared by either roasting or grilling. In Cuba one can try *fufu*, a type of stuffing made with bacon, onion and ripe plantains. Argentina and Uruguay have a penchant for *buñuelos de banana*, banana fritters made with a traditional sweet pastry. In the Caribbean islands plantains are used as a versatile ingredient, cooked at different stages of ripeness, and prepared either salted, fried – both savoury and sweet – or as an additional ingredient in local curries. It is not too ambitious to say that, thanks to their adaptability and culinary colonization of different areas in the world, bananas have united cultures and people that could not seem further apart, geographically and anthropologically, but which have found a common ground in the culinary idiom of the ubiquitous fruit.

When still green, and very starchy, bananas and plantains can even be dried and ground to make flour, an ingredient that finds a number of culinary uses and is a popular feature in the cooking repertoire of West Africa and Jamaica. Due to the high starch content of the green fruit used, banana flour does not actually taste like bananas. In fact, banana flour has an earthy and mellow flavour, more reminiscent of wheatflour products than the 'fruity' staple it comes from. Banana flour is more efficient in its usage, with 25 per cent less volume needed to produce a loaf of the same weight when compared to ordinary wheat-based milled flours. This important characteristic explains its historical identification as a 'poor food', preferred for the feeding of lower social groups in plantation economies, where bananas grew in abundance and with minimum expense. This, of course, is a legacy of the banana's uses in West Africa, where it had been a cheap and important ingredient for large families for centuries. Banana flour also contains no trace of gluten, which explains its recent popularity in the West as an ingredient for those suffering from coeliac disease. The Wedo brand of banana flour has capitalized on this selling potential by labelling itself as a 'healthy, gluten-free food', and attracting the attention of several groups of consumers wanting to lead a 'clean lifestyle', often of the 'paleo' (paleolithic) diet persuasion.

Banana Splits

The banana split is, perhaps, one of the most widely known ways to prepare bananas; the dish has a high iconic value, reminiscent of ice cream parlours in the United States in the 1950s, an image undoubtedly encouraged by numerous examples in popular culture over the years. For this reason, the banana split deserves to be considered as an extremely important incarnation of the banana at work, with all the national and cultural connotations that come with it. The banana split is an ice-cream-based dessert, served, in its most recognizable form, in a long dish, most commonly made of glass, known as a 'boat'. Many variations of the dessert exist. Traditionally, however, the recipe calls for the banana to be cut or 'split' in half lengthwise, and laid in the middle of the dish. Ice cream is then added, the classic incarnation made with scoops of chocolate, vanilla and strawberry, served in a row. Toppings of strawberries, pineapple slices and chocolate sauce are then added, piled as high and as plentifully as the prospective eater desires. Other popular additions to the toppings list include nuts, maraschino cherries and, of course, whipped cream.

Drink a Banana promotional campaign from Dairy Queen, *c.* 1930s.

Like other famous sweet banana recipes known in the West, the banana split finds its origins in the United States. The first banana split was served at Tassel Pharmacy, a small drug- and candy store, in Latrobe, Pennsylvania, in 1904. The inventor of the dessert was David Evans Stickler, a 23-year-old apprentice pharmacist, who was known to enjoy experimenting with sundaes and various drinks, served at the store's soda fountain.[6] Stickler's creation was the classic banana-based, triple ice cream sundae, then served with chocolate sauce as the only topping. The first banana splits retailed at 10 cents each. The dessert's lush and colourful appearance quickly caught the eye of local schoolchildren and high-school students, and it was not long until the popularity of 'the split' reached far beyond the town limits of Latrobe.

An official and popular recipe for the banana split was circulated in *Merck's Report: A Practical Journal of Pharmacy as a Profession and a Business* in 1907, and called for mountains of whipped cream, chopped nuts, chopped dried fruits and a single maraschino cherry on top as additional toppings, giving the banana split its long-standing, iconic look.[7] In a very short period of time the banana split's popularity grew tremendously and, by the 1920s, the dessert was served in almost all ice cream and soda fountain establishments across the States. The city of Latrobe holds an annual celebration to commemorate the famous dessert; this takes place in the form of the renowned, and pointedly named, Great American Banana Split Festival. In 2004 Latrobe also celebrated the 100-year anniversary of the invention of the banana split, hosting an even greater version of the festival, where banana splits were served in all manners of different ways, from the classic recipe

Banana split, served with the traditional whipped cream and chopped nuts, as well as the more recent addition of chocolate sauce.

to contemporary incarnations served with marshmallows, chocolate and even peanut butter. This was also the year when the National Ice Cream Retailers Association certified Latrobe as the banana split's official birthplace, solidifying the city's claim to the famous dessert.[8]

Although Stickler is officially accredited as the creator of the banana split, when the dessert gained popularity at a national level others also laid claim to its invention. The city of Wilmington, Ohio, provides such an example. It is rumoured that in 1907 the local restaurant owner Ernest Hazard staged a culinary contest to attract the attention of the students at nearby Wilmington College. The winner is said to have been his own creation: a banana cut lengthwise and served with ice cream.[9] While it is no one's intention to deny Mr Hazard's culinary talent, the later date of the story unfortunately places his moment of culinary creativity behind Stickler's experimentation. Nonetheless, the town of Wilmington still feels a close affiliation with the famous banana dessert, and celebrates it with a Banana Split Festival, held every year in June.

Banana Bread

In culinary folklore it is a commonly accepted fact that 'banana bread' first made its appearance during the years of the Great Depression in the United States (c. 1930–40). Following the economic crash of 1929, the country was left in dire straits; in a very short period of time the majority of people employed in manual labour, especially those in the Southern states, were out of work. By 1933 over a third of non-farm workers in the country were unemployed. In underprivileged urban areas unemployment soared. This was a time of frugality, when food scarcity was unfortunately the order of the day, and very little, if any, public assistance was offered to the out-of-work labourers and their families.[10] Hunger and malnutrition became common, and it was clear that the situation called for all available foods to be used efficiently and with the greatest nutritional gain. It was during this time that banana bread found its way to success, more out of ingenuity and necessity than culinary frivolity.[11]

The first printed recipe for banana bread appeared in *Balanced Recipes*, a spiral-bound collection of recipe cards published by Pillsbury in 1933 and collected by Mary Ellis Ames, then the director of Pillsbury Cooking Services. Although there is no evidence to confirm that an American cook had not experimented with putting bananas in bread before this time, Ames's collection was the first to formally acknowledge its possibility. It is rumoured that the recipe was intended to encourage American housewives to use all manner of foods available in their deprived kitchens to make everyday staple

Banana bread, as prepared in the traditional loaf tin.

foods, such as bread. As bananas become overripe very quickly, the temptation to throw them away would be high, but waste was not advisable at a time of such austerity. The high nutritional value of bananas made them a welcome addition to the list of ingredients, and the easy and quick nature of the recipe made for an immediate popular favourite. Banana bread is as popular today as it was then, so much so that National Banana Bread Day is celebrated on 23 February in the United States. And while the 'holiday' may not be celebrated by many, its very existence attests to the important part that bananas have played in constructing the pages of culinary history for the nation, even during times of difficulty.

Banoffee Pie

When banana cakes and other sweet treats come to mind, it is virtually impossible not to think of the now almost ubiquitous banoffee pie. A famous recipe that uses sweet bananas, the banoffee pie has become a recurrent presence on dessert menus at restaurants of all persuasions, as well as a beloved family dish to be consumed at home. The banoffee pie is an English dessert made of simple ingredients: bananas, cream and toffee, the latter made from boiling condensed milk. The banana, toffee and cream combination sits on a pastry base, although some variations on the traditional recipe suggest the use of a base made from crushed biscuits – usually digestives – and butter. Chocolate and sometimes coffee sauce are also sometimes added as toppings. The most important ingredients in the pie are highlighted in the very name of the dish, with 'banoffee' a portmanteau of the words 'banana' and 'toffee'.

The origins of the banoffee pie can be traced to the town of Jevington, East Sussex, where Ian Dowding and Nigel

Banoffee pie, served with a chocolate topping.

Mackenzie – the chef and owner, respectively, of The Hungry Monk restaurant – have been credited with its invention. Dowding and Mackenzie claim to have developed the idea of the banoffee pie in 1971. They assert that it was inspired by Jane Dowding, Ian's sister, who, having learnt the many uses of canned condensed milk once it is transformed into toffee, shared her enthusiasm with her brother and Mackenzie, sparking their creativity. The story goes that Mackenzie came up with the idea of putting bananas, toffee and cream together, and suggested to Dowding that the three ingredients could be combined to make a new dessert. Dowding took on the challenge and, after experimenting with a number of different bases, went on to create the banoffee pie. Although this was the original name, Mackenzie later insisted on changing the official name to 'banoffi pie' in an attempt to make the dessert sound more sophisticated.[12] Despite his efforts, however, the spelling of 'banoffee pie' stuck, and this is how it is most commonly written, even today. In truth, the spelling 'banoffee' makes a lot more sense in view of the dessert's ingredients, so it is not difficult to see why the preference for this version of the name has not waned.

The dish was an immediate hit at the restaurant and constantly in demand with customers; what began as a special quickly became a fixed presence on the menu. The official recipe for banoffee or banoffi pie was published for the first time in *The Deeper Secrets of the Hungry Monk* in 1974, with a reprint in the much later *In Heaven with The Hungry Monk* (1997). In between the publication of the two cookbooks, however, the popularity of banoffee pie grew exponentially and many restaurants, as well as cookbooks and households, adopted it as a regular feature. It began to appear on menus throughout the English-speaking world.[13] Global companies such as Nestlé also capitalized on the connection between bananas and toffee, often by affixing a recipe for banoffee pie to the tins of their condensed milk. The dessert became so well known that in 1984 a number of supermarkets in the United States began to sell it as an 'American pie'. Indeed, many chefs in America claimed that banoffee pie had originated in their country, and not at The Hungry Monk. Outraged by the claim, in 1994 Mackenzie issued a challenge with a prize of £10,000 to anyone who could prove the existence of a written and recorded recipe for banoffee pie prior to the publication of their 1974 version.[14] When the search did not return any favourable entries, The Hungry Monk's claim as the birthplace of the dessert was confirmed and a blue heritage plaque commemorating its invention was affixed upon the walls of the restaurant. Sadly The Hungry Monk closed its doors for good in 2012. Nonetheless its culinary legacy remains, and the banoffee pie claims the title of being one of the most famous and cherished uses for the banana in contemporary Western cuisine.

3
The Banana Trade

Bananas have been commercially grown, transported and sold around the world for centuries. Records show that a form of banana trade was already clearly developed as early as 1000 BC in India, its reach extending as far as Malaysia and parts of Indonesia. These operations were, however, mainly the occupation of merchants who transported and sold bananas on a relatively contained scale. As time went by, and capitalism took hold of different types of market economy, many companies experienced a rise and fall in their fortunes, and some focused on localized import and export ventures that only made available small quantities of bananas, considered luxuries for the rich. From the late nineteenth century onwards, however, when new transportation and refrigeration technologies changed the food business trade forever, banana commerce experienced a boost in growth and expansion.

Of all the 'banana companies' in the world, and especially of those providing bananas to the West, three have maintained high levels of success. These are Chiquita (originally known as United Fruit), Dole (the contemporary name of Castle & Cooke) and Fyffes, an Irish fruit company founded and still headquartered in Dublin. This is not to say, of course, that these are the only 'banana companies' in the world, as several

Advertisement for the Fruit Dispatch Company, *c.* 1920s.

exist both within and outside the bounds of Euro–American commerce, with names such as Del Monte and, recently, the Chinese group Xiamen Great Rise leading the way. Nonetheless, and in spite of the competition, Chiquita, Dole and Fyffes remain unavoidable names when discussing the international banana trade. These giant corporate groups have worked to expand their empires so much that they now own and operate, in a shared manner, the great majority of the banana trade in the United States and Europe. With all their success, however, comes a level of controversy, and these banana companies have been at the centre of disputes and political debates about their dealings throughout the history of their operations.

Banana Companies

The United Fruit Company was arguably the biggest and most controversial banana company in the history of the trade.

The company was founded in 1899 and was the result of a merger between Minor C. Keith's banana enterprises and the Boston Fruit Company. Keith had begun dealings in banana plantations in 1877, when he had found himself in Costa Rica managing a project building railways throughout the country.[1] Keith decided to use bananas as a cheap source of food for his workers, emulating the efforts made by slave plantation owners in the Caribbean decades before. His banana interests moved him to establish banana plantations in Panama and in the Colombian Magdalen Department; he founded a reasonably successful commercial entity trading bananas, named Tropical Trading and Transport Company, which operated out of New Orleans and transported bananas back to the United States via what is now the Caribbean port of Limón.[2] Finding himself in financial trouble and on the verge of bankruptcy, Keith travelled to Boston in 1899 to oversee a new business venture: the merging of his banana trading company with the Boston Fruit Company, owned by his rivals Lorenzo Dow Baker and Andrew W. Preston, who had been trading bananas out of Jamaica since 1870. Rebranded as the 'United Fruit

Loading bananas, from a New Orleans postcard, postmarked 1917.

Jamaican women carrying bananas, 1940.

Company', the business kept its headquarters in Boston, with Preston as president. The company grew to be extremely successful, and in a very short period of time it became one of the primary banana traders in the United States, acquiring many plantations in Central and South America, as well as Jamaica. By 1930 the United Fruit Company had absorbed numerous competing banana firms and become the largest plantation employer in Central America. This was also the year when Sam Zemurray, famously nicknamed 'Sam the banana man', sold his successful Cuyamel Fruit Company – operating in Honduras – to United Fruit, retiring a very rich man.[3] In 1933, however, Zemurray became concerned with what he saw as a clear mismanagement of United Fruit and staged a hostile takeover of the company. Once in charge he relocated the company's headquarters to New Orleans and went on to make United Fruit an even more prosperous enterprise. At this time, and for most of its history, United Fruit's main competitor in the United States, as well as other parts of the world, remained the Dole Food Company.

In 1968 Eli M. Black became the largest stakeholder of United Fruit and in 1970 he went on to merge it with his own public enterprise, AMK, to form what became known as the United Brands Company. After Black's takeover, however, the company plunged into significant financial difficulties and found itself in crippling debt. The difficulty of the financial situation experienced by United Brands was aggravated by the occurrence of Hurricane Fifi in 1974, which destroyed several of their banana plantations in Honduras, pulverizing any source of profit for the company. In the midst of political controversies, which accused United Brands of bribery and lobbying in both Central America and the United States, Black committed suicide in February 1975. After Black's death the American Financial Group, led by Carl Lindner Jr, bought United Brands and commenced its return to commercial success.

As a commercial and later corporate group, United Fruit and United Brands have often been at the centre of much criticism and have been accused by various social and political groups of exploiting their plantation workers in Central and South America through a form of neocolonialism. A large number of books, ranging from historical to business analysis and cultural critique, have been written about the dealings of the United Fruit Company. The view of the corporation in this research has remained invariably negative, and United Fruit is often used as a synonym for the exploitation of workers and unsustainable working conditions in the banana trade. The reputation for exploitation has also been heavily criticized by journalists, novelists and artists alike. In 1950 Gore Vidal published the novel *Dark Green, Bright Red*, in which a banana company supports a military coup in an imaginary Central

American country; the novel is often argued to be a very thinly fictionalized rendition of United Fruit's intervention in the political uprising in Guatemala. The continuous political lobbying of the company in Central and South America also led to several uprisings in their plantations, where army intervention caused the deaths of many of those involved. Possibly in an attempt to distance the company from its negative international reputation, in 1985 Lindner decided to change the name of United Brands to Chiquita Brands International. If the rebranding was indeed intended to remove the corporation from highly political discussions over its dealings – an intention that Chiquita have never confirmed – then the move proved unsuccessful. The trade mistakes of United Fruit were never forgotten; this was also probably aided by the fact that Chiquita continued for a long time on the same path as its predecessor. The reputation of having a lack of business integrity continues to haunt the image of the company, in spite of their efforts to revolutionize it in the eyes of the public. Still, Chiquita remains one of the most successful banana companies in the world and one of the key producers of the fruit in the global economy.

A constant competitor to Chiquita's market interests, the Dole Food Company is another American-based multinational corporation, which was founded in 1851 and headquartered in Westlake Village, California. The company finds its origins in the establishment of the import–export company Castle & Cooke, established by the missionaries Samuel Northrop Castle and Amos Starr Cooke in Hawaii. Under the name of Castle & Cooke, the company quickly rose to success, becoming one of the largest businesses in Hawaii. At this time, the company was not solely focused on trading fruit, but counted investments in several business areas, including railway construction, seafood packing and sugar production.

United Fruit advert, 1950s.

Castle & Cooke remained a successful independent company for over 50 years.[4] In 1901 James Dole founded the Hawaiian Pineapple Company, which would later become an important part of the Castle & Cooke business venture. Dole opened his first pineapple plantation on the Hawaiian island of Oahu. He rapidly found success in the trade and the Hawaiian Pineapple Company soon became a household name.

The success of Dole's enterprise did not fail to attract the attention of other business owners and in 1932 Castle & Cooke purchased a 21 per cent share in the Hawaiian Pineapple Company. Dole's original company remained partially owned by Castle & Cooke until not long after James Dole – dubbed the 'king of pineapple' by historians Linda K. Menton and Eileen H. Tamura – died in 1958.[5] In 1961 Castle & Cooke purchased the totality of the Hawaiian Pineapple Company and took over full control. At the same time they also purchased the Standard Fruit Company, a business based in New Orleans and responsible for the commercial sale of a number of exotic fruits into the United States, with bananas a particularly successful item. Business was profitable for both Castle & Cooke and Dole's company, especially after the annexation of Hawaii to the United States in 1959 allowed agricultural produce coming from the islands to be sold on the mainland without paying import taxes. Castle & Cooke decided to merge the two fruit companies and rebrand the single business as the Dole Food Company, Inc. Under this new name, Dole became the third largest producer and importer of bananas based in the United States. Dole is currently still one of the

Bobby Banana, the Dole mascot, as it appears on their packaging.

top banana companies in the American continent, sharing the control of the banana market with Chiquita. Dole is in charge of operating plantations of bananas, as well as other tropical fruits, throughout South and Central America, as well as in the Asia-Pacific regions, counting both plantations and packing establishments in the Philippines and Thailand.[6]

Over the years, Dole has established its place not only as a business entity, but as a cultural one. The mascot of the Dole Food Company is Bobby Banana, an anthropomorphic banana who continues to appear in games and comics for children and who is also the leader of the 'SuperKids' – the children who regularly eat at least five fruits and vegetables each day.[7] The reach of Dole into the cultural sector also expanded into the world of sports when, in 1985–6, the Dole banana was

Sundrop bananas advertising figure, *c.* 1960s.

featured as the official fruit of the athletic programmes of Pittsburgh State University, known collectively as the Gorillas. The appeal of the banana as one of the symbols for the team was not difficult to recognize and Dole was happy not only to offer the sponsorship, but to capitalize on the commercial success that resulted from the promotion.

On the other side of the Atlantic, both Chiquita and Dole have had steady opposition in the form of Fyffes plc. Fyffes was founded in 1888 by Thomas Fyffe, a food wholesaler from London who established a partnership with banana dealers operating in the Canary Islands.[8] At the time, the company was known as 'Fyffe & Hudson', also including the surname of Fyffe's business partner. Although Fyffes has dealt in a variety of fruit during its time, it has always been mainly known for its banana cargos, the first of which reached England under the name of Fyffe the same year the company was founded. Within the first years of operation Fyffe set up multiple banana plantations in the Canaries. In 1901 Fyffe & Hudson merged with Elder Dempster & Company, a shipping firm that had been transporting bananas from Jamaica to the British Isles for a number of years. The company that emerged as a result was renamed Elders & Fyffes, and was aided in its business set-up by the British government, which agreed to pay a subsidy of £40,000 a year to the company in order for them to establish a regular steamliner from Jamaica so that bananas could be made available and sold in greater quantities in Britain.[9] Soon after the merger took place, United Fruit, Elders & Fyffes' American competitor, purchased 45 per cent of the company's capital. In spite of weakening the businesses, however, the inclusion of United Fruit in the Elders & Fyffes' stock allowed the company to grow exponentially and granted them use of specially constructed ships that made the Atlantic crossing easier on the precious banana cargo. In the midst of

Fyffes bananas, promotional rubber handgun from Belgium, 1950s.

financial success, the famous blue label of the company was
used for the first time in 1929.[10]

Elders & Fyffes were known to be particularly keen on
experimenting with new transportation and refrigeration techniques. In 1960 the company partnered with Britten-Norman
Ltd – a British aircraft manufacturer – and agreed to trial the
new 'Cushioncraft' air vehicle to air freight bananas from
multiple regions in West Africa. In 1969 the company was
renamed Fyffes Group Ltd, the name by which it is still known
today. Fyffes relocated its headquarters to Dublin after the
takeover by Irish group FII plc in 1986. The company has
enjoyed a reasonably stable political and financial climate, with
the biggest exception being a court case in 2002 when Fyffes
took legal action against DCC Ltd – an Irish investment group
– with claims of insider trading. After long-drawn-out legal
proceedings, the Supreme Court of Ireland ruled in favour
of Fyffes, declaring a civil settlement that cost DCC over 42
million Euros, equivalent to U.S.$52 million.

Fyffes advertisement, 1940s.

Fyffes offer the public a full range of bananas, which are sourced from multiple plantations in tropical countries, such as Costa Rica, Brazil, Colombia, Ecuador and Honduras. It handles the entire banana export production for the country of Belize, a monopoly that grants the company a virtually unbeatable business advantage. Unlike other banana companies, especially those in United States, Fyffes has striven to maintain a favourable public profile and disassociate itself from the claims of worker exploitation and neocolonialism that have dogged the history of banana companies for almost two centuries. This is in spite of the fact that the company was owned by Chiquita for almost a century and was, at least on paper, associated with the other corporation's turbulent history. Fyffes, however, has been openly keen to recognize the efforts of subsidiary companies in the tropics and has made public announcements over its mission to offer its employees decent working conditions and a decent wage. In 2008 Fyffes proudly announced a corporate philanthropic partnership with UNICEF Ireland. The partnership will fund UNICEF's work in Mozambique fighting the spread of malaria among vulnerable children.[11] These efforts have greatly aided the public image of Fyffes as an 'ethical' company, as close to the idea of 'fair trade' as a corporation could be. The full reality of this public relations campaign remains to be seen, but it does not hurt to stay hopeful that in a fair-minded and impartial banana company exists in the world.

The fates of the three giant banana companies, Chiquita, Dole and Fyffes, have been profoundly entangled for almost the entirety of their existence. Following the end of the Second World War, Chiquita became Europe's main banana provider, exporting to Germany as well as Great Britain and other countries.[12] Chiquita diversified its import sources in order to adapt to European demands; while Germany, among others, permitted the primary inflow of bananas from Latin America, Great Britain, together with France, gave preference to bananas originating in their former colonies in Africa, the Caribbean and the Pacific – also known as the ACP regions. Chiquita was happy to oblige, as its plantation empire allowed it to provide bananas from all these areas. In 1986, however, believing in its dominance over the European market, Chiquita sold its shares of the Fyffes subsidiary, which at the time was the company's primary marketer of bananas from ACP countries. Chiquita was confident that the newly formed European Union of the early 1990s would only mean an increase in sales for its business and, anticipating a growing market, it took on more production facilities in Latin America, which put the company hugely in debt. In the beginning this move proved to be successful and by 1992 Chiquita's European market share was more than double that of Dole and its hold over the German market amounted to over 40 per cent.

Nonetheless, the fate and success of Chiquita in Europe was soon to change. In 1993 the newly formed European Commission restricted the import of bananas from Latin America in favour of produce coming from ACP providers.[13] Clearly this proved a severe blow for Chiquita's interests and the company began a very costly and aggressive lobbying campaign with the U.S. government, denouncing what it claimed to be a discriminatory policy on the European Union's part. Following Chiquita's efforts, the World Trade Organization did indeed declare the European banana policy to be prejudiced and ordered its dismantlement. The EU, however, was not keen to comply, and what followed was years of international disputes, often known as 'the banana wars'. In spite of its debates and continuous lobbying with the U.S. government, which continued to plunge the company into even greater debt, by 1995 Chiquita's limited ability to export ACP bananas into Europe had cost the company a third of its market in that area. The financial consequences for the banana giant were truly disastrous. Meanwhile, Chiquita's main competitor Dole was able to capitalize on the European restrictions on banana imports. The company increased production from its ACP producers and expanded its European market share to 16 per cent.

Eventually the EU did yield and agreed to reopen the sale of banana originating from Latin America into its countries.

The move, however, came with many constraints and arrived far too late to save Chiquita from tragedy. Crippled by debt and loss of market share, Chiquita filed for bankruptcy in 2001. The company re-emerged in 2002, but the road to regaining success has been slow and arduous. The twist of fate for the company happened over ten years later and materialized in the form of an old business partnership. In early 2014 Fyffes and Chiquita agreed to a stock merger, with a purchase of assets being valued at U.S.\$526 million. The merger has made ChiquitaFyffes plc the biggest 'banana company' in the world, making competition to this newly established financial giant virtually impossible on the global market.

The Banana Wars

The production of bananas via corporate organizations has been at the centre of controversies for over a century. One of the key points in the debate has been the ethical – or to be more precise, unethical – treatment of workers in banana plantations; over the years this has covered not only the inadequate conditions in which the workers were forced to operate, but the barely existent remuneration that they would receive for their labour, forcing them into a life of poverty in spite of their hard work, while feeding the corrupt interests of the dictators in so-called 'banana republics'. This appellative refers to economically disadvantaged and politically unstable countries whose economy is largely and almost singularly dependent on the production and export of a product classed internationally as 'rare' and coming from limited-resource areas. Geographically speaking, countries that are classified as 'banana republics' include several countries in Central America, Guatemala and Honduras in particular. Although several items of produce fall into the category, historically bananas have been the primary source of national income for these countries, hence the name.

The term 'banana republic' originated in studies in political sciences and was coined by the American writer William Sydney Porter, who is often known by his pen name O. Henry. He created the term to describe the characteristics and workings of the fictional Republic of Anchuria in his contentious book *Cabbages and Kings*, published in 1904. The book comprises a collection of thematically connected essays that were inspired by Porter's experiences during his stay in Honduras between the years of 1896 and 1897. The Republic of Anchuria does not emerge as a successful country in Porter's writing, and it is plagued not only by corruption and embezzlement, but by a truly unhinged, laughable economy that depends on the production and sale of exotic fruits like bananas. Following Porter's work, and after it was appropriated for wider use by political analysts, the expression 'banana republic' has been used pejoratively to refer to countries that are operated by either dictatorships or oligarchies and which are socioeconomically based on the exploitation of agricultural workers who operate the industry of banana cultivation and export. The term is also used in situations where those in power deal closely with (often) international corporations to generate revenue not for the country overall, but for their own interests. Banana republics are often understood as being motivated by the economic and political collusion between the state and their favoured industrial monopolies, so that the return of private profit not only overrules but completely obscures the needs of the country's wider population. This situation commonly results in enormous financial debts for the country itself, which are – unlike the possible profits – seen as the responsibility of the whole group of workers, who are

How the right care of BANANAS will increase winter profits!

Compliments of
J. A. TRIMBLE & CO.
123 E. Third St.   Bethlehem, Pa.

Informational booklet encouraging potential investors to become involved in the banana trade, 1928.

heavily taxed on their already meagre wages and therefore never allowed to rise and prosper, feeding the stratification of classes within the national scale. Such an imbalance in the running of social, economic and political systems causes 'banana republics' to have a devalued national currency and therefore a non-existent presence in international economies; other countries will not recognize them as functioning financial entities and will therefore not offer any form of financial support in the form of credit.[14]

In this context, and in view of the primary place it occupies in numerous discourses for these economically unstable countries, it becomes inevitable to see the banana not only as a financially tainted entity, but as a symbol of the exploitation of the working masses in favour of the profit of a few, in areas where agricultural production is the only source of national income. Needless to say, the symbolism extends to seeing the banana at the centre of debates over commercial greed, where Western corporations exploit the vulnerable and the exposed in areas of the world that are often unprotected by international laws. The discussion over working conditions in banana plantations has been fomented not only by simple philosophical debates, but by the actual repercussions of the tensions between workers and plantation owners and the place international corporations have occupied in perpetrating the subjugation of agricultural labourers. The repercussions of these tensions have peaked in violence on a number of occasions over the years; the inevitable loss of lives that resulted from this violence has earned the banana trade its reputation as a gruesome and vicious business.

A famous instance of violence in banana plantations which is particularly despicable and has, unsurprisingly, attracted a lot of attention not only from the media, but from human rights groups, is known as the 'banana massacre', or *matanza de las bananeras*.[15] This took place on 6 December 1928 in the town of Ciénaga, near Santa Maria, Colombia. It involved the killing of an unknown number of plantation labourers working for the United Fruit Company (as it was then known). The banana pickers went on strike at the very beginning of December 1928, the principal reasons for which concerned the lack of appropriate working conditions, labour regulations and a remuneration system that was based on actual funds, rather than food coupons. The strikers were led by five leaders – Pedro del Río, Bernardino Guerrero, Raúl Eduardo Mahecha, Nicanor Serrano and Erasmo Coronel – and demanded not only proper pay, but written contracts and the establishment of regulated eight-hour work days in a six-day working week. The strike received the support of a number of left-wing political parties in Colombia – such as the Liberal, Communist and Socialist parties – which even joined in the protest. The strike became the centre of much civil unrest, which alarmed political and trade groups alike. Although a brave and hopeful manoeuvre on the banana pickers' part, the strike was obviously a disruptive action for the plantations and quickly received a response from American-owned United Fruit. The strike openly threatened the corporate interests of the company and had the potential to cause serious financial losses to the group.

Nonetheless, instead of attempting reconciliation with their plantation workers and granting them what many of us would regard as the minimum for leading a decent human life, United Fruit lobbied the American government at the time – led by President Calvin Coolidge – to send troops to Colombia and end the strike, so that production could resume. Needless to say, the landing of American troops on Colombian soil would have represented a disastrous event as far as international politics, as well as economies, were concerned. In a bid to avoid the intervention of the u.s. Army in the matter, the Colombian government acted to suppress the strike by sending its own army, led by General Cortés Vargas. Once the Colombian troops arrived at the site of the strike in the main square of Ciénaga, the situation quickly took a turn for the worse. The banana pickers refused to disperse and, instead, stood their ground. This was viewed as a subversive action by the army and its reaction was unfortunately astounding. Soldiers closed off access to the main street adjacent to the central square, and machine guns were set up on the roofs of surrounding low buildings. By this point, the square was filled not only with the workers of the banana plantations, but with their wives and children, who had gathered to be with them after Sunday Mass; they formed a dense group whose numbers were large and unknown.[16] The troops issued a laughable five-minute warning to the people in the square, after which, at the order of General Vargas, they opened fire on the crowd. The result was carnage.

After the massacre, General Vargas took responsibility for 47 casualties, though the actual number of victims remains undocumented. The political historian Herrera Soto claims that, according to testimonies from survivors collected at the time of the massacre and subsequent documents leaked from the Colombian governments, the number of casualties could have been as high as 2,000.[17] General Vargas continued to maintain that the shooting of the banana plantation workers was a necessary action for avoiding conflict with the American government, which was poised to defend the American personnel of United Fruit, as well as the interests of the company. He argued that the ending of the strike, even by violent means, ensured the safety of Colombia as a country and avoided an American invasion. This position was not fully supported by the Colombian government. Senator Jorge Eliécer Gaitán, for instance, heavily condemned the shooting and claimed that bullets used on the helpless civilians could have been put to better use by being pointed at the (potential) American aggressor. United Fruits, for their part, remained silent in the matter after the massacre was carried out; new workers were found for the plantations and production quickly resumed.

The company never denied nor accepted any responsibility for the actions carried out by the Colombian government and the deaths that resulted from them.

In spite of United Fruit's desire not to address the incident, news of the massacre quickly spread and reached the ears of several activist movements not only in the United States but across the world. Although it is far from the only occurrence of its kind, the 'banana massacre' is often remembered as one of the definitive moments in history in the identification of the banana trade as corrupt and possibly in breach of human rights. A fictional version of the massacre was immortalized by Gabriel García Márquez in his novel *One Hundred Years of Solitude* (1967); another fictionalized version of the events appears in Álvaro Cepeda Samudio's *The Great House* (1962). Activism connected to the banana industry, which solidified at the end of the twentieth century and gave birth to the fair trade movement, is testament to the international cultural shock caused by events such as this. The activist Harriet Lamb maintains that, as far as banana commerce is concerned, the fair trade initiative can only be successful if it is run by 'perfectly ordinary people' who wish to 'transform' the industry and make it 'more visible in our shops, media and local communities'.[18] The banana massacre, therefore, remains not only as a memory, but as a warning for future generations.

Bananas in the South Pacific

The origin of bananas in the South Pacific has left an indelible mark on the relationship that countries in this region have with the fruit today. The importance of the banana in people's lives and economies is not just a legacy, but a living presence. From the Solomon Islands to Fiji, the Cook Islands and Samoa, bananas are a significant agricultural product and many cultivar varieties of the fruit are available, ranging from green to red and yellow. Some Pacific countries have capitalized on the production of bananas for international export, so that the crops are not just a local culinary presence, but an essential part of local economies. Some of these countries, such as Fiji, have been at the centre of disputes over their reinvention as the 'banana republics' of the South Pacific, a point of discussion that has generated many controversies over the years. The Fijian journalist Geraldine Panapasa has traced several issues of financial instability in the economy of the country to the corruption within local banana commerce, controversially claiming that Fiji has become nothing more than a ghost 'living in the shadow of the banana trade'.[19] Nonetheless, other areas of the South Pacific have been more fortunate in their development of banana economies, aided primarily by the efforts of international agricultural safeguarding and fair trade groups.

American Samoa is currently one of the big producers of bananas in the South Pacific. Several farms are located on the main islands of Aunu'u, Ofu, Olosega and Ta'u, producing bananas for both the domestic and export markets.[20] The primary variety of banana grown in American Samoa is the popular Cavendish, with varieties such as the Bluggoe and Mysore – known locally as *Fa'i Pata* and *Fa'i Misi Luki* – coming close behind. The latter, however, is mainly consumed locally and not reserved for the international market. The production of bananas in American Samoa took a turn for the better in the early 1990s, when the Department of Agriculture agreed to expand the development of commercial farms. At this time the local government also invested in growing bananas, which were to be included in school lunches. In July 2001 the department banned the importation of bananas from other areas, including the neighbouring (Western) Samoa (commonly referred to simply as 'Samoa'), in order to protect the market for local growers.

In Samoa bananas are the main agricultural product, followed closely by taro and coconuts. Indeed, bananas and taro are important parts of the Samoan diet and have been for many centuries, if not millennia. In *An Account of Samoan History*, published in 1918, the eminent historian Te'o Tuvale wrote about the food supply in Samoa and reported that the banana, known locally as *Fa'i*, is 'a staple food and forms a part of any and all meals'. Tuvale goes on to say that Samoans prefer 'to cut the fruit when green and bake or boil it'; the fruit is then prepared in various other ways.[21] Tuvale records several traditional ways of preparing and eating bananas in local Samoan dishes, including *masi*, where breadfruit and bananas are buried in the ground until fermented and consumed in a similar manner to cheese; *oloolo*, green bananas grated and mixed with coconut milk and baked; and *poi*, ripe bananas cut up and mixed with coconut milk as a salad. Variations of these dishes can still be found in the culinary repertoire of Samoa today. Traditionally the economy of Samoa has been dependent on agriculture, fishing and, more recently, tourism, so the commercial growth and export of bananas plays a very important part in the local economy. Samoa has capitalized on the growth of 'organic' bananas, establishing itself as an important exporter of this produce to countries such as New Zealand. The important partnership with Kiwi wholesalers, supported by organizations such as Oxfam and the All Good Organics food company, has revitalized the Samoan banana trade, placing a particular emphasis on the exchange of 'rare' banana products such as chunks of dried *misiluki* bananas, produced locally in Samoa and sold in New Zealand in health shops and delicatessens.[22] Previous efforts had been made to

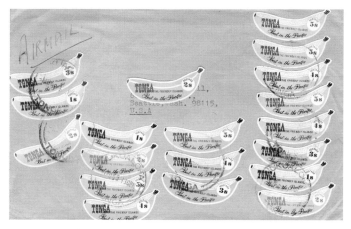

Banana-themed stamps from Tonga, 1969.

import fresh *misiluki* bananas, but this variety, although sweet and delicious in taste, does not travel well and the experiment failed when entire cargos of *misilukis* reached the shores of New Zealand completely black. The attempt to export and sell dried *misiluki* chunks has, on the other hand, been much more successful. Most commercial entities in Samoa also famously operate a fair trade policy in their banana plantations in an effort to sustain local economies and their place in international markets.

Samoa, however, is not the only country to have established a close partnership with New Zealand within the banana export channels. Historically Tonga has been very successful in producing plentiful banana crops and exporting them to New Zealand. Like other areas in the South Pacific, the culinary culture of Tonga features several important uses for the banana, making it once again a staple ingredient. Although the local consumption of bananas has always been high, in the 1950s Tonga began a venture to grow and export bananas to their Kiwi neighbours. The Tongan government set up a system of economic support, known as the Produce Board, for local growers to develop commercial plantations of bananas aimed at export. The bid was successful and the production and sale of bananas increased greatly throughout the 1950s and '60s. In 1963 the success of the banana trade was even celebrated in Tonga with the release of the now famous self-adhesive 'banana stamps'; these items paid tribute to the place occupied by bananas in Tonga's economy, as well as its social structures.[23] Unfortunately a wave of plant diseases in the 1970s affected the Tongan production of bananas for the international market and its industry took an incredible hit. Thanks to the great efforts of the local agricultural board, as well as the aid received by international entities, Tonga's production of bananas in contemporary times has been rejuvenated and continues to flourish, even if the high quantities of produce achieved in previous decades have not been replicated and the consumption of these bananas is mainly domestic. Still, bananas remain an essential part of Tongan life and an unavoidable cultural presence.

4
Imaginary Bananas

Images of bananas have adorned a variety of objects – from clothing to musical instruments – as well as appearing at the visual centre of cultural narratives for centuries. One need only visit the Banana Museum in the town of Auburn, Washington, to realize the extent to which the banana has conquered popular culture. Upon entering the museum – which holds over 600 items, an impressive and surprising number – one is presented with a gigantic array of whimsical objects that have the banana as the inspirational image at their core: banana-shaped phones, plates, costumes and musical instruments are but the beginning of what is on offer.[1] Bananas appear on T-shirts and tins, while innumerable toys and figurines also take the form of the popular fruit. Spanning over 200 years of history, the Washington Banana Museum pays testament to the hold the banana has had over Western consciousness for centuries. Bananas have truly been an omnipresent icon in popular culture, as well as in the world of art, and they can appear in the most bizarre and incredible places. Beyond the bounds of the museum, one does not need to travel far to encounter the image of a banana in what seem like unlikely places. So many examples exist, in fact, that it is virtually impossible to mention them all and this is not a task that I am

Items on display at the Banana Museum in Auburn, Washington.

even willing to attempt. Nonetheless, some examples of 'imaginary bananas' in the last two centuries are particularly worthy of note and deserve special attention as their important place in popular culture is re-evaluated.

Bananas in Popular Culture

In the late Victorian period and well into the twentieth century, the banana was a popular item to be used in celebratory and commemorative products. Numerous examples of postal and birthday cards emerged during this period in which scenes of people eating bananas encapsulated ideas of joy and prosperity, as well as the fun times inevitably evoked by a fruit that was seen as coming from free-loving and easy-going exotic areas. Bananas inspired paintings by Paul Gauguin, Giorgio de Chirico and Salvador Dalí, to mention but a few. Throughout the twentieth century, the perceived 'fun' nature of the banana continued to be exploited and reiterated, when many examples in popular culture, from music to television and comics, used the image of the banana.

'Yes! We Have No Bananas' is a whimsical song written by Frank Silver and Irving Cohn, originally presented in the Broadway revue *Make It Snappy* and first performed in 1922. In the original theatrical performance the song was sung by Eddie Cantor. Following the success of the revue, the song became a hit in 1923, conquering the charts at number one for five weeks. Although the musical historian Arnold Shaw has labelled the song 'derivative in title and melody',[2] 'Yes! We Have No Bananas' grew into an exceptionally successful novelty song of the time, becoming one of the most recognizable tunes in the United States and, arguably, much of the Western world. The version of the song that was released in the charts was actually recorded by Billy Jones, with the vocal support of Arthur Hall and Irving Kaufman. The lyrics of the song are unassuming and entertaining, with a touch of the cultural stereotyping that was unfortunately a popular addition at the time:

BIRTHDAY WISHES

Of all the days of all the year
That bring their joys to you,
May this your birthday bring you dear
The best you ever knew.

Cabaret girl, from a set of two birthday postcards dated late 1890s and early 1900s.

Little girl, from the same set of two birthday postcards.

KINDEST REGARDS
ON YOUR
BIRTHDAY.

Best love on a greeting card
Wishes sincere and kindest regard.

There's a fruit store on our street
It's run by a Greek
And he keeps good things to eat
But you should hear him speak!
When you ask him anything, he never answers 'no'
He just 'yes'es you to death, and as he takes your dough
He tells you
'Yes, we have no bananas
We have-a no bananas today
We've string beans, and onions

Cabashes, and scallions,
And all sorts of fruit and say
We have an old fashioned to-mah-to
A Long Island po-tah-to
But yes, we have no bananas
We have no bananas today.'³

The song also had a less successful but still well-known musical sequel in 'I've got the Yes! We Have No Banana Blues', recorded in 1923 by Billy Jones and his performing troupe. The inspiration for the song is generally attributed to a well-known banana shortage in Brazil, caused by an epidemic of blight. The actual origin of the song goes back to Lynbrook,

Postcard from 1909. The original picture of 'boy with a banana' was a studio portrait by celebrated photographer Reuben R. Sallows.

'Yes! We Have No Bananas' sheet music, 1923.

a small town in Long Island, New York, where – it is claimed – the songwriters composed the lyrics after hearing the words 'Yes! We have no bananas' being uttered by Jimmy Costas, a local Greek American greengrocer.[4] An article from the *Chicago Tribune* dated July 1923, however, claims that the phrase originated in Chicago in 1920; the *Tribune*, unfortunately, does not present much evidence for this claim and fails to provide any form of association between the city of Chicago and anyone having a concern about banana shortages. The Long Island origin is the most widely accepted one, as several witnesses of the time claimed to have heard Mr Costas shoo away eager customers in search of bananas by using the now famous catchphrase.

Both the song and the catchphrase 'Yes! We Have No Bananas' have found popularity over the decades, going well beyond simple entertainment purposes. Indeed, what was once a jolly song in a comedic sketch, performed as part of a theatre revue, became used as a slogan with distinctive political undertones. On the various occasions on which the popularity of the tune was resurrected in history, the bananas in the song ceased to be about consuming food and took on metaphorical meanings. The song was resurrected as the theme of the Outdoor Relief protests in Belfast in 1932; in this case, the shortage of bananas is said to have evoked the depression and sadness that pervaded the city of Belfast at the time, as a tumultuous place lacking happiness and satisfaction.

The banana catchphrase continued to be revived during times of difficulty. It found renewed popularity during the food shortages and rationing periods in the United Kingdom during the Second World War, when the British government decided to ban the import of bananas for a number of years. At the time, the banning of bananas was ill-received by both national and international groups. On the international scale, the ban on bananas meant the breaking of a long-standing trade agreement between the British Empire and numerous banana producers from the Caribbean, causing much unrest and straining political relationships. At home, the ban on the fruit became synonymous with the strife of the war effort, the noticeable absence of the banana on fruit carts being symbolically interpreted as the lack of peace and well-being.

Even beyond its brief political interludes, the song 'Yes! We Have No Bananas' has found fame in multiple examples of popular culture over the decades, keeping alive in the wider cultural psyche the use of the banana as a symbol of contentment and pleasure. The song was part of a storyline in the immensely popular *Archie* comics – a series in which bananas appear on a number of occasions – and it has been mentioned in numerous films, from *Sabrina* (1954) to *The English Patient* (1996). In these cinematic examples, the resurgence of the 'Yes! We Have No Bananas' song is usually associated with moments of extreme joviality, a nod not only to the cheery tune of the song itself, but to the continuous association of the banana with good times. The joviality of the banana symbol was also reiterated via the famous tune in numerous television shows, with notable examples including famous sketches on *The Muppet Show* and *Sesame Street*, as well as on the immensely popular television show *The Simpsons*, in an episode entitled 'Bart's Girlfriend', where the character Homer briefly sings the song. These are but a few examples of the song being resurrected for numerous purposes. These pay testament to the popularity of the song and its adaptability, conveying messages of desire, joy and scarcity – showing how bananas easily become the emblematic messenger for a variety of feelings.

The cultural use of bananas as popular icons continued throughout the 1940s and '50s. Bananas were often included in performance numbers and popular songs, released both as individual musical pieces and as part of film soundtracks. Bananas continued to maintain an association with the exotic, as well as represent a leisurely lifestyle and sensual experiences. A famous example of this was the now iconic 'Day-O', also known as the 'Banana Boat Song', performed by the

Jamaican American singer Harry Belafonte in 1956. The song was originally a well-known Jamaican *mento* song – a traditional style of folk music using acoustic elements such as the banjo and hand-drums, often regarded as a subcategory of the more famous calypso music – but Belafonte's version popularized it for the Western world, becoming one of his signature pieces. In keeping with the thematic stylings of *mento* music, 'Day-O' is a typical work song, narrating the everyday occurrences of dock workers loading bananas onto ships. The musical historian Chris Bebenek claims that, in spite of the success of the single, which sold a staggering 1.5 million copies at the time, Belafonte was accused of 'bastardizing' true calypso music in order to adapt it to American tastes.[5] Others, however, have praised the song for being particularly attuned to the hard work that banana loading requires and the desire of the workers to go home and rest at the end of the day. After the success of Belafonte's single, many other versions of the song were recorded in the years that followed. A famous example was the one sung by Stan Freberg in the 1950s and later picked up in the mid-1980s as the theme song for the chocolate bar Trio in its UK advertising. Belafonte's version, however, continues to be remembered as the 'original', probably in view of the cultural connection between the song as being of Jamaican origin and Belafonte's own Jamaican heritage. This association was also proudly picked up by Shaggy, another Jamaican singer, when he released a dance-inspired version of the song on his 1995 album *Boom-bastic*. The 'Banana Boat Song' has also been used on several occasions as part of television and film soundtracks, most famously for the 'possessed' dinner sequence in Tim Burton's *Beetlejuice* (1988).

During the 1960s bananas took on different figurative meanings in the West and in the popular culture of the United

States in particular. A famous instance of experimentation with the banana as metaphor during this time is Andy Warhol's contentious cover art for the self-titled debut album of The Velvet Underground & Nico. This artistic rendition of the banana is possibly one of the most recognizable and iconic pictures of the fruit in popular culture. The cover shows the painted picture of a simple banana, which is slightly bruised and blackened at the edges. Early copies of the album actually invited people to 'Peel slowly and see'; the album owners that were tempted by the invitation would be presented with a different picture of the banana re-releasing its inner flesh-coloured self. The 'peel and see' version of the cover was a technically challenging product to create; a specially designed machine was needed to manufacture the cover, which increased the production costs of the album significantly.[6] The album cover was conceived and released in 1966 in the middle of Andy Warhol's Exploding Plastic Inevitable media tour, and displayed many of the experimental characteristics of image and concept that have become known as part of Warhol's distinctive art sensibilities of the time. The image of the peeled banana was suggestively sexual and at the centre of many sociopolitical controversies of the time, so much so that later versions of the cover no longer presented the double-edged offer of peeling off the skin to the prospective purchaser. In 2012, over 50 years since it was first released, Warhol's banana image was involved in a lawsuit between the Velvet Underground business partnership and The Andy Warhol Foundation for the Visual Arts. The Velvet Underground partnership sued the Warhol Foundation after it openly licensed the album cover's iconic banana design to Incase Designs for reproduction on iPhone and iPad cases. After several hearings over the ownership of the trademark design, in March 2013 the court dismissed the partnership's claim and facilitated a settlement between the two parties.[7] It is curious to think that, decades after it was produced and released, Warhol's iconic banana continued to be at the centre of controversies, even if the litigations were more financial than sociopolitical and sociocultural in nature.

Donovan sang about bananas in his 1966 hit 'Mellow Yellow'. The song's lyrics claimed that the banana would be able to provide 'electric effects'. Donovan's song was released in the midst of a subcultural trend of smoking the scraped and dried innards of banana skins, in the belief that this would allow the willing smoker to begin a journey into an alternative world, 'seeing' what others could not see.[8] In truth, the banana is able to produce only minor effects on the brain that replicate feelings of happiness and excitement. The reason for this has less of a spiritual and more of a biochemical – and perhaps mundane – origin. Bananas contain many sugars and provide a lasting source of energy for the body. These sugars are also able to lift the mood of the consumer and can provide a sense of serenity or, if consumed in higher quantities, a distinct wave of euphoria. These results are attributable to the fact that consuming the sugars contained in bananas is known to aid the production of dopamine and seratonin in the brain, often allegedly recalling the effects on neurotransmitters caused by Ecstasy and Prozac.[9] Of course, it is not being suggested that bananas are in any way comparable to any medically developed mood inhibitors; nonetheless, the high sugar content of the fruit could bestow a sense of well-being to those who eat it, even if it is for a very short time. The counterculture of the 1960s was clearly onto something when it recognized the potential effects of the banana, even if attributing pseudo-hallucinogenic properties to it may have been going a bit too far.

The banana's potential to change one's mood, however, was not a new idea that sprang up as part of the counterculture of the 1960s. The fruit's mood-altering properties had been recognized in the West long before, undoubtedly spurred by stories and legends coming from the East. In 1935 the *Oxford English Dictionary* established the expression 'going bananas' as an entry associated with insanity.[10] The expression is still in use today to refer to someone going 'a little bit mad', even with extreme happiness, or by becoming overly passionate over an incident and indulging in public displays of emotion. In *The Historical Dictionary of American Slang*, the lexicographer J. E. Lighter also claims that there is an association between the expression 'going bananas' and its counterpart 'going ape', which became more prevalent in the mid-twentieth century. Both signify being irrational and overreacting to a particular situation. Lighter contends that when considered together the expressions may allude to the close cultural association of primates and monkeys eating bananas, and that one phrase may have developed as an elaboration of the other.

Going Bananas was also the title of a superhero comedy series produced by Hanna-Barbera and broadcast only for a short period of three months in 1984. The series starred James Avery and told the story of Roxana Banana, an orang-utan who escaped from a zoo and was adopted by the Coles family. The twist of the story was that, on a special night, a mysterious spaceship landed in the backyard and endowed the orang-utan with superpowers. Roxana, while still maintaining a healthy dose of ape-like behaviour and a distinct love of bananas, then developed her role as a crime-fighting ape; the hilarity and silly situations caused by this development provide much of the comedy of the series. *Going Bananas* only ran for a short period of time, but over the years gained cult status. This is, of course, in spite of the series' ludicrous premise and low production values. Its title helped to keep the use of the eponymous phrase alive – the show truly is a little bit crazy

The popular word game Bananagrams includes a well-known 'going bananas' play on words in its slogan.

– as well as re-establishing the cultural association between bananas and apes.

In the world of children's popular culture, bananas have occupied a prominent place as the stars of the popular *Bananas in Pyjamas*, an Australian television show that ran originally from 1992 to 2001 and was then resurrected for a brief period, running from 2011 to 2013. The concept of the show was inspired by the successful song 'Bananas in Pyjamas', written and performed by Carey Blyton in 1967, and featured on *Play School*, an educational children's show broadcast on Australian television; the song was later chosen as the theme tune for the series. The main characters of *Bananas in Pyjamas* are, unsurprisingly, two anthropomorphic bananas named B1 and B2, the names clearly inspired by prominent vitamins that make up the banana's chemical composition. The two bananas wear striped blue-and-white pyjamas and live happily in a quiet property on a road called Cuddles Avenue, a tranquil neighbourhood they share with a group of three teddy bears and the oddly conspicuous Rat in a Hat. Being Australian, the bananas indulge in culturally common, although slightly stereotypical, Australian activities: they live by the ocean and operate as the local beach patrol. 'Yellow jelly' is the main characters' favourite food and, like many aspects of the series, its contents and meanings are left unexamined – including why, indeed, the bananas should have such a penchant for wearing pyjamas. Since the launch of the series, the bananas' catchphrases of, 'Are you thinking what I'm thinking, B1?' and 'I think I am, B2', have become part of the linguistic repertoire of a whole generation of television watchers. Over time *Bananas in Pyjamas* has gathered a fan base that goes way beyond the Australian shores; the series was syndicated in 1995 and modified and redubbed in order to reflect the local nuances of the countries in which it was broadcast. Notable among the changes was the modification of the title in the United States to mirror the local spelling of 'pajamas'. Although unarguably strange, the series proved very successful and cemented the place occupied by the banana in the children's world of contemporary popular entertainment.

Though the story of giant bananas strutting around on a sunny beach wearing pyjamas and enjoying the company of rats seems odd enough, other twentieth-century children's stories have also centred on bananas and have maintained a healthy dose of oddity, coupled with a shade of political critique. One of these was *Bananaman*, a British comic strip and later an animated cartoon series, created by Dave Donaldson and Steve Bright and developed by John Geering. *Bananaman* was first published in *Nutty* magazine in February 1980 and was clearly a parody of adult superhero stories, especially *Superman* and *Batman*, but also with a touch of *Marvelman*.[11] The strip tells the story of Eric Wimp, a rather ordinary schoolboy living at 29 Acacia Road, in the town of Nuttytown – later renamed Dandytown, after the disappearance of *Nutty* magazine and the publication's switch to *The Dandy*. When Eric eats a banana he transforms into Bananaman, an adult superhero who proudly displays a tight blue and yellow outfit – which we now recognize as the trademark colours of Chiquita bananas – complete with a yellow cape that, unsurprisingly, resembles a banana peel. Bananaman's superpowers include super strength, the ability to fly and invulnerability to nearly all weapons. Bananaman does not need to worry about running out of strength or endurance, for if he finds himself in need of extra power he can simply eat more bananas, which will provide an immediate boost. The bananas are delivered to him by his faithful and ever so slightly sarcastic pet crow. Indeed, bananas are the answer in all of Bananaman's endeavours, providing all the physical top-up he might need. As a boy Eric is constantly bullied but as a banana-eating superhero he is strong and full of energy, ready to conquer all his foes. It is quite obvious that *Bananaman* sits somewhere between commercial advertising, genre parody and anti-bullying propaganda, encouraging children to eat healthy snacks, which became synonymous with strength and independence. The touch of British humour in the series is commendable, as is its ability to subtly make fun of its own imagery. In *Bananaman*, one can see once again how socio-political narratives were constructed in popular culture via the seemingly humble image of the banana.

In recent years bananas have made an iconic appearance in the world of fashion by becoming a favourite motif in the designs of the Italian high-fashion label Prada. Banana prints were the motif of choice of the fashion house in 2011, appearing on numerous examples of skirts and blouses. Prada's chief designer Miuccia Prada described the banana print as 'minimal baroque', praising the bold nature of the banana as an image with connotations of 'slapstick humour'.[12]

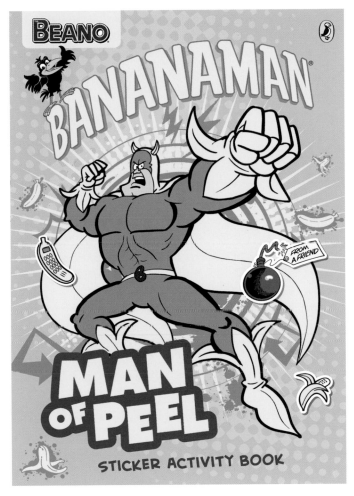

Bananaman sticker activity book.

Prada's interest in the banana image pays testament to the fruit's continuous connection to joyous desires, and overly sensuous and potentially sexual experiences, which find their most fitting incarnation in the unassuming and discreet appeal of the everyday.

Sexy Bananas

The symbolic association between bananas and sex is said to have begun in Western popular culture in the nineteenth century. The phallic shape of the banana was noticed almost immediately as its popularity spread in the prim and proper Victorian world, when endless jokes and illustrations suggestively connecting the consumption of bananas with sexual intercourse were disseminated and enjoyed. At one point, bananas were even at risk of being targeted by temperance groups as an overly 'sexy' fruit that brought with them the suggestion of illicit behaviour. To counteract the obvious sexual suggestiveness of the banana, in the late 1890s banana companies such as United Fruit and Fyffes began to circulate promotional postcards of prudish ladies consuming the fruit both in the United States and Europe.[13] The straight-laced nature of the pictures was meant to eliminate the sexual connotations of the fruit and encourage its consumption in temperate circles. The circulation of the postcards was complemented with the endorsement of numerous cookbooks that included creative ways of preparing bananas, in an attempt to promote the fruit as a wholesome family food. The propagandist move only partially had the desired effect; undoubtedly the association with bananas and women of good morals heightened the profile of the fruit and allowed it to be viewed as 'safe'. Nonetheless, the temperate campaign on bananas also inevitably drew even more attention to the fruit's phallic shape and its association with the sexual act continued to be prevalent.

In the late nineteenth and early twentieth centuries bananas became the visual epitome of exotic lands, which were inevitably thought to hold the secrets of erotic pleasures and desires. Indeed, the postcards depicting prim images of banana-eating ladies found a viable opponent in another set of materials which actually emphasized the banana's 'sexy' appearance. Several postcards originating from the United Kingdom in the late Victorian period, and even later into the following century, made suggestive references to the banana's 'sexy' connotations, often using the idea of 'having a banana' as a euphemism for having sex. The association between bananas, exotic lands, leisure and developed sexual appetites maintained a strong hold over Western depictions of Africa, South America and the Caribbean for a long time, cementing itself into the Western cultural imagination and often becoming accepted as a universal truth.[14] One can see these depictions stretching well into the twentieth century, when the sexualization of the female body and the sexualization of the banana became one. This relationship often relied on offensive and derogatory racial stereotypes, where examples of popular culture such as prints, songs and musical numbers relied on depicting individuals originating from Africa as having unusually heightened sexual desires.

In spite of the worrying racial stereotyping of these images, some performers were able to use this depiction in their act and display it with grace. The most famous example of this kind is to be found in Josephine Baker's famous performance of the 'banana dance'. Baker was an African American singer, dancer and actress who became famous for her sexy and titillating performances, which later earned

Poster for *Clockwork Banana*, a French low-budget movie of 1973.

her the names 'Black Venus' and 'Black Pearl'. She was primarily active as a performer in the 1920s and '30s, when she toured the United States and Europe. Baker's performances gained her immediate notoriety, as she was known to present herself almost nude on stage, engaging in extremely erotic moves and dances to music. Her rise to fame in the early 1920s in France was primarily due to her now canonically famous 'banana dance', during which she appeared on stage wearing only a skimpy bikini top and a bottom adorned by small artificial bananas, which would leave very little to the viewer's imagination. As Baker danced frenetically across the stage, her bananas would dangle provocatively from her hips. Baker openly indulged in the image of the 'sexy African' and in her performances often portrayed herself as a 'dark-skinned savage' climbing trees, which fed into the white European fascination with the oldest continent.[15] Although many have viewed Baker's performances as an example of racial subjugation and continuous typecasting, others have seen her as a figure of female emancipation. The eroticization of the banana, in this context, can be viewed as symbolic of the sexual emancipation of a woman who takes control of her desires and pursues them as she wishes. Symbol of female emancipation or not, Baker's banana dance and costume remain one of the most iconic uses of bananas in popular culture, emphasizing their multiple uses and incarnations within the world of entertainment.

In the late 1920s and '30s sexy and appealing images of the banana, coupled with attractive young women, continued to pervade popular culture, often following in Baker's footsteps but not always managing to capitalize as effectively on her appeal. An example of this was the release of the 1929 film *His Captive Woman*, directed by George Fitzmaurice and starring the distinctly Caucasian Dorothy Mackaill. In one

Josephine Baker performing the 'banana dance' in her famous banana skirt, 1927.

heavily publicized scene from the movie Mackaill wears a banana skirt that is clearly reminiscent of Baker's stage costume. The skirt, however, is much more subdued, in that the number of bananas has increased, forming many layers that definitely look more like a full garment, almost reaching the actress's knees – a definitive change from Baker's 'skirt', which sported one single line of bananas and made for a far sexier look. Nonetheless Mackaill's own version of the banana dance was still an attempt at sexualizing the female body through an association with a 'sexy' and exotic fruit and, if nothing else, a clear attempt at colonizing the sensual female dancer in a more culturally appropriate, 'Western' way.

The 'banana dance' phenomenon started by Josephine Baker is not the only example of the banana being sexualized, or at least holding a connection to matters of a sexy nature, within popular culture. Another famous instance of this is to be found in the Chiquita banana, also known as 'Miss Chiquita'. Miss Chiquita was launched in 1944 by the Chiquita company – then still United Fruit – as part of its rebranding and in an effort to offer a distinctive logo and 'face' that would make the enterprise recognizable to the public. The debut of the Miss Chiquita banana began with the launch of the Chiquita banana jingle, arguably one of the best-known advertising jingles of all time.[16] The tune was written by the company's advertising agency, led at the time by creative director Robert Foreman and his co-workers, who developed the jingle by using the combination of an old piano and box of paper clips shaken to simulate the sound of maracas.[17] Chief lyrics director Garth Montgomery wrote the lyrics for the famous jingle, while Len Mackenzie provided the music. The singer for the original 1944 recording of the jingle was Patti Clayton, the first to embody 'Miss Chiquita' in a long line of performers. Even today, the lyrics of the song are very recognizable; they lie somewhere in between advertising and educational instruction on how to look after bananas as a product.

> I'm Chiquita banana and I've come to say
> Bananas have to ripen in a certain way
> When they are fleck'd with brown and have a golden hue
> Bananas taste the best and are best for you
> You can put them in a salad
> You can put them in a pie-aye
> Any way you want to eat them
> It's impossible to beat them
> But, bananas like the climate of the very, very tropical
> equator
> So you should never put bananas in the refrigerator.

After the jingle first hit the radio airwaves, it is estimated that at the peak of its popularity it was played over 370 times a day on radio stations across the United States. The Chiquita song proved instantly successful, due to its unavoidably catchy tune. The jingle had a distinctive Latino sound to it, which was meant to evoke exotic notions of the lands where the bananas came from. In spite of its seemingly helpful advice, however, it is essential to point out that the information the jingle provided was actually wrong: as the historian Virginia Scott Jenkins points out, the United Fruit company was known to have multiple cold-storage rooms across America in which they refrigerated bananas.[18] Still, it would have been a shame to ruin such a craftily composed tune by providing useful advice that would potentially lower the sales numbers for the company. The error was, therefore, never addressed.

The Miss Chiquita jingle, however, was not simply a catchy song. It functioned as the launching pad for the 'real' Miss

Chiquita, the new face of the company: an animated dancing and singing banana, wearing a sexy and colourful red outfit, complete with a ruffled skirt and a bowl of fruit on her head. It is neither difficult, nor ambitious, to guess that Miss Chiquita was modelled on the Brazilian actress Carmen Miranda, who had been known to wear similar outfits in her musical performances and who was a hugely popular cinematic figure at the time. Miranda herself was also known for surrounding herself with bananas as she performed her exotic dances; a famous examples of this is the 'Tutti Frutti' routine she performs in the film *The Gang's All Here* (1943), a bright cinematic extravaganza in which she seductively struts around a plantation in a faraway land, arriving into the scene sitting on a giant cart full of bananas. One can see here the entanglement between the food world of the banana and the networks of popular culture, proving that, when it comes to cultural history, the connections between areas of human performance and engagement run deep. Miss Chiquita danced seductively and sang with a distinctively 'exotic' accent and, in so doing, heightened the attraction of the banana as both a food and an experience. It is incredible to think that the humble banana could be bestowed with any kind of sex appeal, but the luscious red lips, seductive black-lined eyes and provocative poses of the Miss Chiquita character begged to differ.

Over the decades Miss Chiquita has headed several campaigns for the Chiquita company, endorsing the sales of several banana-based products, from cookbooks to memorabilia like phones and aprons. While very little has changed as far as the appearance of Miss Chiquita is concerned, her jingle was given a makeover in 1999, when the misinformation about refrigeration was removed and a few more of the lyrics were modernized to reflect contemporary concerns:

The iconic image of Carmen Miranda singing amid bananas in the film *The Gang's All Here* (1943).

I'm Chiquita Banana and I've come to say
I offer good nutrition in a simple way
When you eat a Chiquita you've done your part
To give every single day a healthy start
Underneath the crescent yellow
You'll find vitamins and great taste
With no fat, you just can't beat 'em
You'll feel better when you eat 'em
They're a gift from Mother Nature and a natural addition
    to your table
For wholesome, healthy, pure bananas – look for
    Chiquita's label!

The Latino sound that made the jingle famous was noticeably toned down in the most recent version, making it a little less sexy and exotic and a bit more homey and inconspicuous.

And while small changes have been applied to the song she sings and the message she delivers, the hold of the Miss Chiquita banana remains strong today; the lady herself has become an iconic part of popular culture, proof that commercial enterprise can quickly bestow upon images a profound contextual significance. A parody of the song was even included in the 2013 film *Despicable Me 2*, performed by the popular Minions who, in emulation of the Chiquita Banana style, even wore fruity headdresses for the occasion. In truth, no other food is as unintentionally sexualized as the banana and the Miss Chiquita campaign successfully made a virtue of this unavoidable and often unspoken fact.

Banana-flavoured Tic Tacs, produced in conjunction with the release of the *Minions* movie (2015).

Miss Chiquita Banana miniature, 1951.

Slipping on a Banana Peel

One of the most well-known examples of the banana in wider popular culture is perhaps its association with physical comedy, in the form of the iconic 'slipping on a banana peel' gag. This comedic stunt has a long-standing history in the use of bananas as part of the performing arts, even though, as historical narratives go, it is a reasonably recent addition. Physical comedy can be credited as one of the oldest forms of comedy. Records show that physical gags date back as far as 2500 BC, when the entertainers of ancient Egypt would slap each other and much hilarity would ensue.[19] Even in this early example, physical comedy would rely on *Schadenfreude*, or the ability to derive pleasure from the misfortune of others. Over the centuries physical comedy evolved to encompass many gags and acts, usually aimed at the satirical representation of particular groups within society, such as the clergy. In the nineteenth century slapstick became the most popular form of comedy, when both British and American comedians turned it into a real work of art. Slipping, smacking and, of course, falling across the stage were seen as the height of comedic performance.

The introduction of the banana peel gag into the repertoire of physical comedy did not happen until the late nineteenth century, and to find its origins we need to travel to the United States. Bananas were first imported en masse into the country in 1866, when the trader Carl B. Frank began an enterprise selling the yellow fruit in the streets of New York City. These bananas originated mainly from Panama and were part of the *Gros Michel* family. Of course, this was not the first time that bananas had reached American shores; in the early nineteenth century sailors returning from journeys in South America had been known to transport back multiple examples of tropical fruits to their homeland. Nonetheless, Frank's enterprise was the first organized venture to import bananas commercially into the United States. At this time bananas were wrapped in foil and sold singly. They proved to be an immediate success with buyers. Curious shoppers would purchase bananas just to take a good look at them, the consumption of the flesh being a lucky by-product of their curiosity. In no time at all, and in spite of the fact that they were not the cheapest snack around, bananas became one of the favourite street foods in circulation.

Thanks to the popularity of the fruit, mixed with a general lack of civic services providing sufficient rubbish bins in several areas of the city, banana skins quickly began to fill the streets and transformed into a nuisance for busy passers-by. The skins would be left in the streets to rot and it was often reported that as they decomposed they would become slippery. With time, the popularity of bananas spread from New York City to other areas of the United States and the 'banana peel issue' became a note of national concern. Public opinion around the issue quickly rose, and the unsightly and potentially dangerous nature of the abandoned bananas peels grabbed the attention of several socially focused publications of the time. In 1879 *Harper's Weekly* magazine included a feature that chastised banana-eaters for tossing banana skins onto the ground with little concern for their fellow man. The magazine claimed that 'whosoever throws banana skins on the sidewalk does a great unkindness to the public, and is quite likely to be responsible for a broken limb'.[20] While the magazine's statement could seem overly sensationalist, even for a popular publication from the late nineteenth century, there is actual evidence of several reported cases in multiple cities across the country of people being taken to hospital with broken limbs, claiming to have slipped on banana skins. Poems and

Vaudeville entertainer Miss Rose Bacon using a banana in her comedy routine, early 1900s.

popular songs began to appear, with the banana at the centre of many people's misfortunes. Limerick-style poems, often of anonymous authorship and sung in the style of a ballad, were particularly in favour:

There was a young lady named Hannah,
Who slipped on a peel of banana.
More stars she espied
As she lay on her side
Than are found in the Star Spangled Banner.

A gentleman sprang to assist her;
He picked up her glove and her wrister;
'Did you fall, Ma'am?' he cried;
'Did you think,' she replied,
'I sat down for the fun of it, Mister?'[21]

The preoccupation with the dangers of abandoned banana skins became so prominent that in 1909 the city of St Louis even outlawed the 'throwing and casting' of banana skins in public. At this time, the presence of banana skins on the streets was certainly no cause for hilarity. Eventually the banana skin crisis in New York City, as well as other areas in the United States, was solved in the very early twentieth century by a public agency headed by former Civil War hero Colonel George Waring, who organized an army of uniformed workers – known as 'the White Wings' – to sweep the streets and dispose of the waste decomposing therein.[22] Nevertheless, and in spite of the efforts made by the local authorities to remove the dangerous skins from the streets, it was not long before the comedic potential of such a worthy fruity fiend would be picked up by successful stage comedians of the time.

The first appearance of the 'banana peel gag' dates back to the early 1900s, right at the time when banana peels were allegedly taking over the streets of American cities. Contemporary entertainer Billy Watson – later known as 'Sliding' Billy Watson – is credited with giving the first ever performance of 'slipping on a banana skin'. Or, at least, Sliding Billy was confident in self-proclaiming himself the inventor of the gag, a claim that has admittedly not been disputed since. It is rumoured that Watson witnessed an unfortunate man slipping on a banana skin and, in spite of the fact the unknown man was reportedly badly injured, the incident inspired Sliding Billy to recreate it as an act for entertainment purposes. The stage performance of the gag soon became a laugh-filled hit and a popular addition to the vaudeville repertory of 'pratfalls', physical comedy acts that focused on the performers falling on their backsides – the term derives from the word 'prat', a sixteenth-century British expression meaning 'buttocks'. At the same time that Sliding Billy was slipping across the floor, a contemporary comedian, Carl Stewart, was also known to have contributed to the popularity of the gag by including several banana-skin jokes as part of his performance as copyrighted and popular persona 'Uncle Josh'. A 1903 recording of the 'Uncle Josh in a Department Store' routine offers several references to slipping on the banana skins that littered the pavements of the cities.

In the early twentieth century the arrival of film provided the ideal medium for the visual entertainment of physical comedy to flourish, with performers such as Charlie Chaplin, Harold Lloyd and Buster Keaton perfecting the art for the screen. These actors capitalized on the appeal of what the film historian Noel Carroll calls a 'mischief sight gag', where watching someone slip on a banana skin involves 'a conflict between the protagonist's unaware interpretation – there is no danger on this sidewalk – and our own awareness of the banana peel'.[23] The silent era truly made a virtue of the banana-skin act. Chaplin is credited with showing the gag on film for the first time in *By the Sea* (1915), where his famous character 'The Tramp' is shown tossing a banana skin on the floor, only to inadvertently slip on it later. In 1917 Harold Lloyd also showed the banana skin as the cause of humorous slippages in *The Flirt*. The set-up in the narrative is simple: Lloyd's character is sitting in a restaurant and after eating a banana he predictably tosses the peel on the floor. A condescending waiter, who had previously judged Lloyd's character on his eating manners, slips on the banana skin and falls comically. An even more developed version of the gag was perfected by Buster Keaton in his film *The High Sign* (1921), where Keaton slips on a banana skin in the street; the gag is successfully aided by Keaton's famous deadpan expression and gifted acting ability, which coupled physical comedy with a highly developed expressive delivery. For many years, if not decades, after the transportation of the banana-skin gag onto film, the act remained a staple of comedic cinema, with other famous performers such as Laurel and Hardy including it in their routines even after sound made its appearance on the silver screen. The 1927 film *The Battle of the Century* is a good example of this, where the banana skin gag is used by Laurel and Hardy as the cheeky and unexpected instigator of a gigantic pie fight, another popular comedic act of the time, taken straight from the physical comedy repertoire. Hardy himself was particularly fond of the banana gag and he is portrayed slipping on a peel in several films, including *From Soup to Nuts* (1927) and *The Hollywood Review of 1929* (1929).[24] More recent re-enactments of the banana skin gag in cinema can be seen in films from *Sleeper* (1973) to *Billy Madison* (1995). And although it is no longer commonly re-enacted in contemporary cinema, the banana-skin gag has remained universally familiar, often coming to stand as a synonym for physical comedy, which takes the slippery nature of the banana skin as a given and unquestionable fact.

In spite of its undying cultural popularity, however, there is very little proof that one banana skin on its own will cause an unfortunate passer-by to slip and fall. A well-known attempt to either confirm or disregard the belief was seen on the television programme *MythBusters*, which aired on the Discovery Channel in 2009. An experiment was set up to test whether banana skins were in fact as slippery as popular culture had given us reason to believe over the years. A single banana skin was set up on the floor and upon walking on it Mythbuster Adam did not manage to slip at all. However, when multiple banana skins were set up on the concrete floor, the unfortunate Adam did indeed slip on them, proving that banana peels can in fact be slippery. The experiment did not confirm that a single banana skin would be slippery at all, or cause falls that would lead to injuries. Still, the potential slipperiness of multiple skins together keeps the myth alive, and one can only show respect for a famous comedic gag that has managed to survive scientific and cultural obstacles for centuries, and remain an important part of Western popular culture. It is perhaps better to continue to imagine the banana skin gag as based in truth, for it would be a shame to give it up as inaccurate when it feeds harmless nostalgia for a bygone era.

Epilogue

Many historians, economists, botanists and activists often refer to the banana as 'the fruit that changed the world'. It is not difficult to see the reasoning behind this claim. Truly, bananas seem to have been entangled with every aspect of the ways in which human society has evolved over millennia of history. Bananas have provided nutrition and culinary flexibility for thousands of years, becoming a staple food of numerous geographical areas and groups, even if the conditions in which they have prospered, and the reasons behind them, have commonly been less than agreeable. Often labelled as 'everyone's favourite fruit', the banana has been at the centre of agricultural and commercial innovations, and it has guided the development of cultures, as well as being at the heart of numerous ongoing controversies.

As a symbol of emancipation and exploitation, sexualization and childhood memories, the banana is more than simply a vehicle for nourishment. Popular and beloved, common and mundane, the banana is a conspicuously slippery entity. The more one searches, the more one finds connections between bananas and the socioeconomic and cultural narratives that create membership as well as animosities. Any account of the banana, global in nature as it might be, is still non-definitive.

The fruit evades any form of conclusive statement in that its cultural importance is constantly changing. As the banana's botanic classification changes, so does its trade and the ways in which it enters people's lives. At best, one can revel in historical snippets; any attempt to mark its development via a linear path ends up in pieces. The banana, it would seem, is a fruit of metamorphosis; it does not have a single 'history', but continues to cyclically flourish and perish in multiple chronicles. Not simply a fruit of the world, the banana hides, instead, the world in a fruit.

Recipes

In spite of the longevity of the relationship between bananas and humans, with the fruit occupying an important place in culinary, cultural and economic narratives, records relaying actual recipes for banana-based dishes are scarce. Prior to the nineteenth century instances of historically chronicled cooking instructions for banana dishes are difficult to find. Nonetheless, the arrival and establishment of the banana in Western culinary organization promoted the insurgence and proliferation of several cookbooks that established the banana as the regular ingredient we recognize today. In these historical sources, as well as in contemporary ones, the banana features mainly as part of sweet or breakfast dishes. It is therefore important to extend the reach of the survey of the banana recipe into cooking manuals that originate from beyond Western countries. The contemporary nature of recipes involving bananas and plantains outside of the United States and Europe – from the Caribbean and the Americas, to Africa and Asia – is inevitable, but it does not detract from highlighting the versatility of the banana as an ingredient and the part it plays in the diet of human beings for both the everyday and the celebratory.

Historical Recipes

Banana Cream

From Mrs F. L. Gillette and Hugo Ziemann, *The White House Cookbook*
(1887)

After peeling the bananas, mash them with an iron or wooden
spoon; allow equal quantities of bananas and sweet cream; to one
quart of the mixture, allow one-quarter of a pound of sugar. Beat
them all together until the cream is light.

Banana Ice

From the Society for Christian Work of the First Unitarian Church,
The Cookery Blue Book (1891)

6 bananas, 3 peaches, 3 lemons, 1 quart sugar, 1 quart boiling water.
Pour hot water over the sugar and lemon juice, and stir until it is
dissolved. When cool add peaches and bananas sliced thin, and let
stand two hours; then strain through fine sieve, so nothing is left
but liquid. Then freeze.

Banana Pudding

From Mary Harris Frazer, *The Kentucky Receipt Book* (1903)

Take ½ dozen bananas, peel and cut in pieces an inch thick, put in
a baking dish and pour over custard made in the following manner:
Custard – One pint of milk, 3 eggs, beat the yolks light, add milk,
also 2 tablespoons of granulated sugar. Have the milk boiling, add
the eggs and let it cook until it thickens; when cool pour over the
bananas. Make a meringue with whites of the eggs and granulated
sugar, put on top of custard, set in oven a few minutes to brown.
Serve at once.

Banana Fritters

From Elizabeth O. Hiller, *Fifty-two Sunday Dinners* (1913)

3 bananas
1 cup bread flour
2 teaspoons baking powder
¼ teaspoon salt
1 tablespoon sugar
¼ cup cream or milk
1 egg beaten very lightly
½ tablespoon lemon juice
½ tablespoon Sherry wine

Sift dry ingredients together twice. To beaten egg add cream and combine mixtures. Force bananas through a sieve and mix pulp with lemon juice and sherry wine; add to batter, beat thoroughly, and drop by tablespoonfuls into deep, hot [oil]. Drain and sprinkle with powdered sugar.

Wholemeal Banana Pudding

From Thomas R. Allinson, *The Allinson Vegetarian Cookery Book* (1915).

2 teacupfuls of fine wheatmeal
3 oz. of sago, 6 bananas
1 tablespoonful of sugar
3 eggs
½ pint of milk

Peel the bananas and mash them with a fork. Soak the sago with ½ pint of water, either in the oven or in a saucepan. Make a batter with the eggs, meal, and milk; add the bananas, sugar and sago, and mix all smoothly. Turn the mixture into a greased mould and steam the pudding for 2 hours.

Modern Recipes

Banana Chocolate Cream Pie

1 cup (200 g) plain (unsweetened) chocolate
2 cups (450 ml) milk
¾ cup (150 g) sugar
5 tablespoons flour
½ tablespoon salt
2 egg yolks, slightly beaten
1 tablespoon butter
½ tablespoon vanilla extract
1 baked 9 in. (25 cm) pie shell
2 very ripe bananas

Melt the chocolate in the milk on the stove top. Beat until blended. Mix the sugar, flour and salt and then add to chocolate mixture. Keep stirring until thickened and completely incorporated. Cook for a further 10 minutes, stirring occasionally. Stir the still hot chocolate mixture into the egg yolks. Cook for 1 minute, then add the butter and vanilla. Set aside and cool thoroughly.

Bake the pie shell and put aside until cool. Spread a layer of the chocolate mixture on the bottom of the pie shell and leave to cool. Add the cut-up bananas as a filling and pour the rest of the chocolate mixture on top until completely covered. Decorate the top of the pie with sliced bananas and serve with whipped cream.

Banoffee Pie

12 oz (350 g) uncooked shortcrust pastry
2 tins (13.5 oz / 400 g each) condensed milk
1½ lb (700 g) firm bananas
12½ fl. oz (375 ml) double (heavy) cream
½ teaspoon powdered instant coffee

1 dessertspoon caster sugar
a little freshly ground coffee

Preheat the oven to 200°C. Line a 25-cm flan tin with baking paper. Spread the thinly rolled out pastry in the tin. Prick the pastry base all over with a fork and bake until crisp. Set aside and allow to cool.

Immerse the unopened tins of condensed milk in a deep pan of boiling water. Cover and boil for approximately 3 hours, ensuring that the pan does not boil dry. The milk will transform into soft toffee during cooking, which will be used as a filling for the pie. After the required 3 hours, remove the tins from the pan of water and allow to cool completely before opening.

Mix the cream with the instant coffee and sugar and whip until thick. Spread the toffee evenly over the pastry base. Peel and cut the bananas into slices and lay them on the toffee. To complete the pie, spoon the cream on top and lightly sprinkle with ground coffee.

Keke fa'i (Samoan Banana Cake)

1½ cups (210 g) flour
1 teaspoon baking powder
¼ teaspoon salt
1 stick + 1 tablespoon (125 g) butter, softened
¾ cup (150 g) sugar
2 eggs
1 teaspoon vanilla
1 cup (200 g) mashed banana (about 2 medium overripe
bananas)
1 teaspoon baking soda
¼ cup (55 ml) hot milk

Line a 20-cm cake tin and preheat the oven to 350°F (180°C). Sift together the flour, baking powder and salt. Set aside. Beat the butter with the sugar until it is creamed to a light and fluffy texture. Continue to beat, adding the vanilla and then one egg at a time until incorporated.

Using a spatula, stir the mashed banana into the butter mixture. Dissolve the baking soda in the milk and add to the mixture. Slowly sift the flour, powder and salt into the mixture and gently fold them in. Once all the ingredients are incorporated, pour the batter evenly into the cake tin and bake for 45 to 50 minutes, or until a toothpick comes out clean.

Lontong (Malaysian Rice in Banana Leaves)

2 cups (400 g) rice
4 banana leaves

Quickly boil the banana leaves until soft. Clean and dry them and then put aside.

Wash and drain the rice. Lay out the softened banana leaves and fill with rice. Wrap the rice in the leaves loosely, achieving tubular pockets of roughly 15 cm in length and 4 cm in width. There must be sufficient space in the pocket for the rice to expand during cooking. Insert a toothpick in the middle of each pocket, in order to keep it fastened.

Place the rice pockets into a large pan filled with water and boil for 3 hours. Do not allow the pan to boil dry. After cooking and cooling, slice the banana-leaf pockets and serve.

Matoke (Ugandan Mashed Green Plantains)

1 cup (250 g) peanut butter
2 cups (450 ml) cold water
2 tablespoons peanut oil
1 onion, finely chopped
salt to taste
ground red pepper to taste
4 green plantains
½ cup (115 ml) boiling water, more if necessary

Place the peanut butter, peanut oil, water and onion in a blender (or food processor). Blend until smooth, making sure all the ingredients are amalgamated. Pour the peanut butter mixture into a small bowl and add salt and ground red pepper to taste. Set aside. Using a knife, slice the plantain skins lengthwise, cutting off both ends and peeling the whole skin off. Cut the inner flesh of the plantains in half, lengthwise. Place the plantains into the top rack of a pan steamer. Fill with water and bring to the boil. Reduce to a simmer, put the lid on and steam for about 15 minutes or until soft. Take care not to overcook the plantains, as they should maintain their texture and consistency. Using a long spatula, transfer the plantains to a medium mixing bowl.

Using a potato masher, pound the plantains until smooth. Add ½ cup of boiling water to the plantains and continue to pound until a mash-like consistency is achieved. Add salt to taste.

Drizzle peanut sauce over the mashed plantains. Serve warm.

Khuy Tod (Thai Fried Bananas)

¾ cup (105 g) rice flour
¼ cup (35 g) tapioca flour
2 tablespoons sugar
1 teaspoon salt
¼ cup (35 g) white sesame seeds
½ cup (40 g) shredded coconut, dried or frozen
¾–1 cup (170–225 ml) water
8 bananas, ripe but firm
3 cups vegetable oil

Mix the flours, salt, sesame seeds, sugar and shredded coconut in a mixing bowl. Add water slowly until the mixture turns into a thick batter. Cut the bananas in half crosswise and then slice the pieces lengthwise into three. Heat the oil in a frying pan over a medium heat. Quickly submerge the banana pieces in the batter and then fry in the oil until golden. Keep turning until the pieces have reached the desired brown colour, then remove from the heat and serve.

Arati Mi Koora (South Indian Plantain Curry)

2 medium plantains
1 tablespoon oil
1 tablespoon chilli powder
1 tablespoon mustard seeds
2 tablespoons dry Bengal gram
2 tablespoons thick tamarind juice
a handful of jaggery
2 green chillies
1 pinch of asafoetida
1 stem of curry leaves
a pinch of turmeric
salt to taste

Peel the plantains and cut them into pieces. Add salt to taste and boil to soften. Strain the plantain pieces and set aside.

In a pan, shallow fry the mustard, asafoetida, dry Bengal gram, turmeric and green chillies in the oil. Add the plantain pieces, together with the curry leaves, chilli powder, jaggery and tamarind juice. Stir and turn as required. When the sauce has thickened remove from the heat and serve.

Stuffed Plantain Boats

2 lb (900 g) plantains, about 6 ripe, firm plantains
½ cup (115 ml) oil
½ cup (60 g) finely grated cheddar (or other) cheese

For the filling:
2 tablespoons olive oil
1 tablespoon butter
1 scotch bonnet or jalapeño chilli, deseeded and minced
2 cloves garlic, minced
½ red pepper, deseeded and minced
½ green pepper, deseeded and minced

8 oz (225 g) minced pork
3 spring onions, green and white parts, thinly sliced
salt and freshly ground pepper

To prepare the filling: in a skillet, heat the oil and butter over a medium heat. Add the chilli and the garlic. Sauté for approximately 30 seconds. Add the peppers and continue to cook until soft. Add the pork and sauté until cooked. Add the spring onions and season with salt and pepper and mix well. Set aside.

Peel the plantains. Heat the oil in a large skillet over a medium heat until hot, but do not allow to smoke. Fry the plantains until golden brown, turning on each side as required. Remove and drain on paper towels. Set aside.

Preheat the oven to 350°F (180°C). Cut a slit into the plantains lengthwise, but make sure that they are not cut into two separate pieces. Fill each plantain with 3 tablespoons of the filling and sprinkle with the grated cheese. Place the stuffed plantains on a baking sheet lined with foil and bake for 20 minutes until they are cooked through. Serve hot.

Banana Banshee

½ fl oz (15 ml) banana liqueur
½ fl oz (15 ml) white crème de cacao
1 cherry
½ fl oz (15 ml) vodka
1½ fl oz (45 ml) cream

Place the banana liqueur, white crème de cacao, vodka and cream into a cocktail shaker and mix well. Strain into a previously chilled cocktail glass. Add the cherry on top and serve.

References

Introducing the Banana Family

1 James P. Smith, *Vascular Plant Families* (Eureka, IL, 1977).
2 Peter Chapman, *Bananas: How the United Fruit Company Shaped the World* (Edinburgh, 2007), p. 13.
3 Scot C. Nelson, Randy C. Ploetz and Angela Kay Kepler, '*Musa* Species: Bananas and Plantains', Species Profile for Pacific Island Agroforestry (permanent resource, 2006). See http://agroforestry.net, accessed 15 November 2014.
4 S. N. Pandey and Ajanta Chadha, *A Text Book of Botany: Plant Anatomy and Economic Botany* (New Delhi, 1993), vol. III, p. 373.
5 Jeff W. Daniells, 'Bananas and Plantain', in *Encyclopaedia of Food Sciences and Nutrition*, ed. Luiz Trugo and P. M. Finglas (Amsterdam, 2003). See also www.growables.org, accessed 20 November 2014.
6 Ibid.
7 Ibid.
8 Pandey and Chadha, *A Text Book of Botany*, p. 373.
9 R. V. Valmayor et al., eds, *Banana Cultivar Names and Synonyms in South East Asia* (Laguna, 2000), p. 2.
10 Ibid.
11 Allen Brodsky, *CRC Handbook of Radiation Measurement and Protection* (West Palm Beach, FL, 1978), p. 620.

12 Dan Koeppel, *Banana: The Fate of the Fruit that Changed the World* (London, 2008), p. xiii.

13 Julia Morton, *Fruits of Warm Climates* (Brattleboro, VT, 1987), p. 31.

14 Koeppel, *Banana*, p. xiv.

15 Ibid.

16 Andrew Nikiforuk, *Pandemonium: How Globalization and Trade are Putting the World at Risk* (St Lucia, 2006), p. 128.

17 A. Barekye et al., 'Analysis of Farmer-preferred Traits as a Basis for Participatory Improvement of East Highland Bananas in Uganda', in *Banana Systems in the Humid Highlands of Sub-Saharan Africa: Enhancing Resilience and Productivity*, ed. Guy Blomme, Bernard Vanlauwe and Piet van Asten (London, 2014), pp. 30–37.

18 Anthony Huxley, *New RHS Dictionary of Gardening* (Basingstoke, 1992), vol. III, p. 268.

19 Katrien Hendrickx, *The Origins of Banana-fibre Cloth in the Ryukyus, Japan* (Leuven, 2007), p. 99.

20 Daniells, 'Bananas and Plantain', p. 377. See also www.growables.org, accessed 20 November 2014.

21 Koeppel, *Banana*, p. xv.

22 Ibid., p. xvi.

23 Ibid., p. xvii.

24 Ernest Small, *Top 100 Food Plants: The World's Most Important Culinary Crops* (Ottawa, 2009), p. 81.

1 Growing Bananas: Histories, Legends and Myths

1 Jeff W. Daniells, 'Bananas and Plantain', in *Encyclopaedia of Food Sciences and Nutrition*, ed. Luiz C. Trugo and Paul M. Finglas (Amsterdam, 2003), p. 373. See also www.growables.org, accessed 20 November 2014.

2 'The World's Top 10 Largest Producer Countries of Bananas', www.countryranker.com, accessed 25 November 2014.

3 See www.australianbananas.com.au.
4 Dan Koeppel, *Banana: The Fate of the Fruit That Changed the World* (London, 2008), p. 15.
5 Ibid.
6 See T. P. Denham et al., 'Origins of Agriculture at Kuk Swamp in the Highlands of New Guinea', *Science*, CCCI/5630 (2003), pp. 189–93.
7 See Jean Kennedy, 'Pacific Bananas: Complex Origins, Multiple Dispersals?', *Asian Perspectives*, XLVII/1 (2008), pp. 75–94. See also http://cwh.ucsc.edu, accessed 20 November 2014.
8 Ibid.
9 Judith Carney, 'Seeds of Memory: Botanical Legacies of the African Diaspora', in *African Ethnobotany in the Americas*, ed. Robert Voeks and John Rashford (New York, 2013), p. 19.
10 Alan Davidson, *The Oxford Companion to Food* (Oxford, 2006), p. 36.
11 Margaret Roberts, *Edible and Medicinal Flowers* (Claremont, CA, 2000), p. 6.
12 Khair Tuwair Said Al-Busaidi, 'Banana Domestication on the Arabian Peninsula: A Review of their Domestication in History', *Journal of Horticulture and Forestry*, V/11 (2013), p. 198.
13 Clifford Thurlow, *The Amazingly Simple Banana Diet* (London, 1995), p. 7.
14 The cubit is an ancient measure of length, usually based on the distance from the elbow to the tip of the middle finger. Various types of 'cubit', measuring different lengths, are known to have been used in the ancient world at different moments throughout history.
15 Quoted in Thurlow, *The Amazingly Simple Banana Diet*, p. 8.
16 Al-Busaidi, 'Banana Domestication on the Arabian Peninsula', p. 197.
17 Ibid., p. 198.
18 Thurlow, *The Amazingly Simple Banana Diet*, p. 10.
19 See Al-Busaidi, 'Banana Domestication on the Arabian Peninsula'.

20 Virginia Scott Jenkins, 'Banana', in *The Oxford Companion to American Food and Drink*, ed. Andrew F. Smith (Oxford, 2007), p. 34.

21 See Carney, 'Seeds of Memory'.

22 Scott Jenkins, 'Banana', p. 35.

23 See Robert Langdon, 'The Banana as a Key to Early American and Polynesian History', *The Journal of Pacific History*, XXVIII/1 (1993), pp. 15–35.

24 Scott Jenkins, 'Banana', p. 34.

25 Jules Verne, *Around the World in 80 Days* (London, 2000), p. 47.

26 Ronald N. Harpelle, *The West Indians of Costa Rica: Race, Class and the Integration of an Ethnic Minority* (Montreal, 2001), p. 15.

27 Scott Jenkins, 'Banana', p. 34.

28 See www.bananamuseum.com, accessed 10 November 2014.

29 Rachel Eagen, *The Biography of Bananas* (New York, 2006), p. 21.

30 Scott Jenkins, 'Banana', p. 34.

31 David Leeming, *A Dictionary of Asian Mythology* (Oxford, 2001), p. 165.

32 Koeppel, *Banana*, p. 3.

33 Ibid., p. 4.

34 Ibid., p. 6.

35 Ibid., p. 7.

36 Theresa Bane, *Encyclopedia of Fairies in World Folklore and Mythology* (Jefferson, NC, 2013), p. 208.

37 William Drake Westervelt, *Legends of Gods and Ghosts: Hawaiian Mythology* (New York, 2014), p. 47.

38 Mellie Leandicho Lopez, *A Handbook of Philippine Folklore* (Quezon City, 2006), p. 158.

39 'Filipino Folktales', www.tagaloglang.com, accessed 20 November 2014.

40 See Nathan Kumar Scott, *The Sacred Banana Leaf* (Chennai, 2008).

41 Daniel J. Crowley, *I Could Talk Old-story Good: Creativity in Bahamian Folklore* (Berkeley, CA, 1983), vol. XVII, p. 82.

42 Daryl Cumber Dance, *Folklore from Contemporary Jamaica* (Knoxville, TN, 1985), p. 26.

2 How to Eat Bananas

1 Virginia Scott Jenkins, 'Banana', in *The Oxford Companion to American Food and Drink*, ed. Andrew F. Smith (Oxford, 2007), p. 34.

2 *Larousse gastronomique* (London, 2007), p. 71.

3 Ibid., p. 72.

4 See Adam Starchild, *The Amazing Banana Cookbook* (Los Angeles, CA, 2004).

5 Ellen Gustafson, *We the Eaters: If We Change Dinner, We Can Change the World* (New York, 2014), p. x. See also Lois Sinaiko Webb, *Multicultural Cookbook of Life-cycle Celebrations* (Westport, CT, 2000), p. 15.

6 Scott Jenkins, 'Banana', p. 35.

7 Theodore Weicker, *Merck's Report: A Practical Journal of Pharmacy as a Profession and a Business* (Whitehouse Station, NJ, 1907), vol. XVII, p. 164.

8 Bruce Steele, 'With a Cherry on Top: Pitt Fetes Alum's Creation of Banana Split', *PittChronicle* (25 August 2004), www.news.pitt.edu.

9 David Hunter, *Day Trips from Cincinnati: Getaways Less than Two Hours Away* (Guilford, CT, 2003), p. 134.

10 See Robert S. McElvaine, *The Great Depression: America, 1929–1941* (New York, 1984).

11 Scott Jenkins, 'Banana', p. 35.

12 'Banoffi Pie', www.hungrymonk.co.uk, accessed 17 November 2014.

13 'The Completely True and Utter Story of the Banoffi Pie', www.iandowding.com, accessed 17 November 2014.

14 Steve Lee, 'Hungry Monk Dishes out the Humble Pie', *The Daily Telegraph* (4 May 1994), www.banoffee.co.uk.

3 The Banana Trade

1 Marcelo Bucheli, *Bananas and Business: The United Fruit Company in Colombia, 1899–2000* (New York, 2005), p. 46.

2 James Wiley, *The Banana: Empires, Trade Wars and Globalization* (Lincoln, NE, 2008), p. 15. See also Ronald N. Harpelle, *The West Indies of Costa Rica: Race, Class and the Integration of an Ethnic Minority* (Montreal, 2001).

3 Rich Cohen, *The Fish that Ate the Whale: The Life and Times of America's Banana King* (London, 2012), p. 101.

4 Pedro Arias, Cora Dankers, Pascal Liu and Paul Pilkauskas, *The World Banana Economy, 1985–2002* (Rome, 2003), p. 75.

5 Linda K. Menton and Eileen H. Tamura, *A History of Hawaii* (Honolulu, HI, 1999), p. 186.

6 See www.dole.co.th, accessed 19 November 2014.

7 'What's a SuperKid?', www.dole.com, accessed 18 November 2014.

8 Gordon Myers, *Banana Wars: The Price of Free Trade* (New York, 2004), p. 5.

9 Ibid., p. 9.

10 'The Fyffes Label', www.fyffes.com, accessed 19 November 2014.

11 'Mozambique President Pays a Visit to Fyffes', www.freshplaza.com, accessed 16 November 2014.

12 Marcelo Bucheli, 'Banana Wars Maneuvres', *Harvard Business Review* (November 2005), wwww.hbr.org, accessed 12 November 2014.

13 Ibid.

14 Mark Moberg and Steve Striffler, 'Introduction', in *The Banana Wars: Power, Production and History in the Americas*, ed. Steve Striffler and Mark Moberg (Durham, NC, 2003), p. 1.

15 Eduardo Posada-Carbó, 'Fiction as History: The Bananeras and Gabriel García Márquez's *One Hundred Years of Solitude*', *Journal of Latin American Studies*, XXX/2 (1998), pp. 395–414.

16 Ana Carrigan, *The Palace of Justice: A Colombian Tragedy* (New York, 1993), p. 16.

17 See Posada-Carbó, 'Fiction as History'.

18 Harriet Lamb, *Fighting the Banana Wars, and other Fairtrade Battles* (London, 2008), pp. 1, 2.

19 'Living in the Shadow of the Banana Trade', *Fiji Times Online*
    (31 August 2008), www.fijitimes.com, accessed
    20 November 2014.
20 See www.ipmcenters.org, accessed 19 November 2014.
21 Te'o Tuvale, *An Account of Samoan History up to 1918* [1918],
    at www.nzetc.victoria.ac.nz, accessed 18 November 2014.
22 'Samoa's *Misiluki* Bananas a Hit with Kiwi Consumers',
    www.theepochtimes.com, accessed 17 November 2014.
23 'The Self-adhesive Stamps of Tonga',
    www.philatelicdatabase.com, accessed 14 November 2014.

4 Imaginary Bananas

1 Washington Banana Museum, www.bananamuseum.com,
   accessed 11 November 2014.
2 Arnold Shaw, *The Jazz Age: Popular Music of the 1920s*
   (New York, 1987), p. 133.
3 This is only the first verse of the song, as written by
   Frank Silver and Irvin Cohn in 1922. See the GEM edition
   published by Shapiro, Bernstein & Co., New York.
4 Shaw, *The Jazz Age*, p. 132.
5 Chris Bebenek, 'Harry Belafonte' in *African American Lives*,
   ed. Henry Louis Gates and Evelyn Brooks (Oxford, 2004),
   p. 65.
6 See Victor Bockris, *Up-tight: The Velvet Underground Story*
   (London, 2009).
7 Scott Mervis, 'Andy Warhol Foundation, Velvet
   Underground Settle Lawsuit over Iconic Banana', *Pittsburgh
   Gazette* (20 March 2013), www.post-gazette.com, accessed
   11 November 2014.
8 Peter Chapman, *Bananas: How the United Fruit Company
   Shaped the World* (Edinburgh, 2007), p. 15.
9 Ibid.
10 Ibid.
11 Becky Parry, *Children, Film and Literacy* (Basingstoke, 2013),
    p. 169.

12 Imogen Fox, 'Prada's Print Bears Fruit', *The Guardian* (29 May 2011), www.theguardian.com, accessed 2 November 2014.

13 Washington Banana Museum, www.bananamuseum.com, accessed 11 November 2014.

14 Krista A. Thompson, *An Eye for the Tropics: Tourism, Photography and Framing the Caribbean Picturesque* (Durham, NC, 2006), p. 74.

15 John Soluri, *Banana Cultures: Agriculture, Consumption and Environmental Change in Honduras and the United States* (Austin, TX, 2005), p. 59.

16 Dan Koeppel, *Banana: The Fate of the Fruit That Changed the World* (London, 2008), p. 116.

17 'The Chiquita Banana Jingle', www.chiquita.com, accessed 3 November 2014.

18 Virginia Scott Jenkins, 'Banana', in *The Oxford Companion to American Food and Drink*, ed. Andrew F. Smith (Oxford, 2007), p. 34.

19 Matt Blitz, 'The Origin of the "Slipping on a Banana Peel" Comedy Gag', www.todayifoundout.com, accessed 4 November 2014.

20 See *Harper's Weekly: Collected Volumes* (1861–1909), vol. IL, p. 1738

21 'Going Bananas', http://guacamolegulch.blogspot.co.nz, accessed 5 November 2014.

22 Koeppel, *Banana*, p. 66.

23 Noel Carroll, 'Notes on the Sight Gag', in *Comedy/Cinema/Theory*, ed. Andrew Horton (Berkeley, CA, 1991), p. 25.

24 Anthony Slide, *The New Historical Dictionary of the American Film Industry* (New York, 2013), p. 19.

Select Bibliography

Bane, Theresa, *Encyclopedia of Fairies in World Folklore and Mythology* (Jefferson, KY, 2013)

Bockris, Victor, *Up-tight: The Velvet Underground Story* (London, 2009)

Bucheli, Marcelo, *Bananas and Business: The United Fruit Company in Colombia, 1899–2000* (New York, 2005)

Carrigan, Ana, *The Palace of Justice: A Colombian Tragedy* (New York, 1993)

Carroll, Noel, 'Notes on the Sight Gag', in *Comedy/Cinema/Theory*, ed. Andrew Horton (Berkeley, CA, 1991), pp. 25–42

Chapman, Peter, *Bananas: How the United Fruit Company Shaped the World* (Edinburgh, 2007)

Cohen, Rich, *The Fish that Ate the Whale: The Life and Times of America's Banana King* (London, 2012)

Crowley, Daniel J., *I Could Talk Old-story Good: Creativity in Bahamian Folklore* (Berkeley, CA, 1983), vol. XVII

Dance, Daryl Cumber, *Folklore from Contemporary Jamaicans* (Knoxville, TN, 1985)

Davidson, Alan, *The Oxford Companion to Food* (Oxford, 2006)

Eagen, Rachel, *The Biography of Bananas* (New York, 2006)

Gates, Henry Louis and Evelyn Brooks, eds, *African American Lives* (Oxford, 2004)

Gustafson, Ellen, *We the Eaters: If We Change Dinner, We Can Change the World* (New York, 2014)

Harpelle, Ronald N., *The West Indians of Costa Rica: Race, Class and the Integration of an Ethnic Minority* (Montreal, 2001)

Hendrickx, Katrien, *The Origins of Banana-fibre Cloth in the Ryukyus, Japan* (Leuven, 2007)

Hunter, David, *From Cincinnati: Getaways Less than Two Hours Away* (Guilford, CT, 2003)

Huxley, Anthony, *New RHS Dictionary of Gardening* (Basingstoke, 1992), vol. III

Koeppel, Dan, *Banana: The Fate of the Fruit That Changed the World* (London, 2008)

Lamb, Harriet, *Fighting the Banana Wars and other Fairtrade Battles* (London, 2008)

Larousse Gastronomique (London, 2007)

Leandicho Lopez, Mellie, *A Handbook of Philippine Folklore* (Quezon City, 2006)

Leeming, David, *A Dictionary of Asian Mythology* (Oxford, 2001)

McElvaine, Robert S., *The Great Depression: America, 1929–1941* (New York, 1984)

Menton Linda K. and Eileen H. Tamura, *A History of Hawaii* (Honolulu, HI, 1999)

Morton, Julia, *Fruits of Warm Climates* (Brattleboro, NC, 1987)

Myers, Gordon, *Banana Wars: The Price of Free Trade* (New York, 2004)

Nikiforuk, Andrew, *Pandemonium: How Globalization and Trade are Putting the World at Risk* (St Lucia, 2006)

Parry, Becky, *Children, Film and Literacy* (Basingstoke, 2013)

Roberts, Margaret, *Edible and Medicinal Flowers* (Claremont, CA, 2000)

Scott, Nathan Kumar, *The Sacred Banana Leaf* (Chennai, 2008)

Sen, Soumen, *Khasi-Jaintia Folklore: Context, Discourse and History* (Chennai, 2004)

Slide, Anthony, *The New Historical Dictionary of the American Film Industry* (New York, 2013)

Small, Ernest, *Top 100 Food Plants: The World's Most Important Culinary Crops* (Ottawa, 2009)

Smith, Andrew F., ed., *The Oxford Companion to American Food and Drink* (Oxford, 2007)

Soluri, John, *Banana Cultures: Agriculture, Consumption and Environmental Change in Honduras and the United States* (Austin, TX, 2005)

Starchild, Adam, *The Amazing Banana Cookbook* (Los Angeles, CA, 2004)

Striffler, Steven and Mark Moberg, eds, *The Banana Wars: Power, Production and History in the Americas* (Durham, NC, 2003)

Thompson, Krista A., *An Eye for the Tropics: Tourism, Photography and Framing the Caribbean Picturesque* (Durham, NC, 2006)

Thurlow, Clifford, *The Amazingly Simple Banana Diet* (London, 1995)

Webb, Lois Sinaiko, *Multicultural Cookbook of Life-cycle Celebrations* (Westport, CT, 2000)

Westervelt, William Drake, *Legends of Gods and Ghosts: Hawaiian Mythology* (New York, 2014)

Wiley, James, *The Banana: Empires, Trade Wars and Globalization* (Lincoln, NE, 2008)

Websites and Associations

Banana Clubs and Associations

The International Banana Club
www.bananaclub.com

International Banana Society
www.bananas.org

World Banana Forum
www.bananalink.org.uk/world-banana-forum

Websites

Chiquita
www.chiquita.com

Dole
www.dole.com

Food and Agricultural Organization of the United Nations
www.fao.org

Fyffes
www.fyffes.com

International Banana Museum
www.internationalbananamuseum.com

UNESCO
www.unesco.org

Washington Banana Museum
www.bananamuseum.com

Acknowledgements

I would like to thank Michael Leaman of Reaktion Books and Andrew F. Smith, the Editor of the Edible series, for giving me the opportunity to write this book. It was a rather enlightening experience. I thought I knew a lot about the cultural and global history of the banana before I began the project, but that turned out to be only half-true.

I'm grateful to Ann Lovell of the Banana Museum in Washington for allowing me to use some the rare photographs of bananas in her collection and for the wonderful work she does in keeping the museum going. I would also like to thank Auckland University of Technology for giving me the time to write this book, and my colleagues and students at AUT for their continued interest in the project (and a good laugh when it was most needed). Special thanks also go to all the researchers in my international academic network for their support and encouragement.

I could never do what I do without the support of my friends and family, to whom I am forever indebted. Above all, my most heartfelt gratitude goes to my husband, Rob Farnell, who always knows how to shine the light whenever I feel deep in the darkness.

Photo Acknowledgements

The author and publishers wish to express their thanks to the below sources of illustrative material and / or permission to reproduce it.

© The Banana Museum, photo Erica MacKenzie: pp. 44, 45, 57, 59, 60, 70, 79, 80, 81, 86, 88, 94, 101, 104, 106, 107, 108, 109, 122, 130, 133; Bananaman ® © DC Thomson & Co. Ltd. 2015: p. 119; © DACS 2015: p. 48; © Lorna Piatti-Farnell: pp. 10, 19, 62, 85, 116, 129; Michael Leaman: p. 58; Shutterstock: p. 6 (Andrejs Zavadskis).

Divya Kudua, the copyright holder of the image on p. 65, Whitney, the copyright holder of the image on p. 73, Glen MacLarty, the copyright holder of the image on p. 75 have published them online under conditions imposed by a Creative Commons Attribution 2.0 Generic license; Charles Haines, the copyright holder of the image on p. 67 has published it online under conditions imposed by a Creative Commons Attribution-Share Alike 2.0 Generic license; Krugen, the copyright holder of the image on p. 64 has published it online under conditions imposed by a Creative Commons Attribution-Share Alike 4.0 International license; German Federal Archives, the copyright holder of the image on p. 42, has published it online under conditions imposed by a Creative Commons Attribution-Share Alike 3.0 Germany license; Thelmadatter, the copyright holder of the image on p. 22, Adam Jones, the copyright holder of the image on p. 31, Frank C. Müller, the copyright holder of the image on p. 63, Arnaud 25, the

Index

italic numbers refer to illustrations; **bold** to recipes